GETTING TO KNOW THE COSMOS

Getting to Know the Cosmos

Hugh Thurston

SERENDIPITY

First published in 2003 by
Serendipity
Suite 530
37 Store Street
Bloomsbury
London
WC1E 7QF

British Library Cataloguing-in-Publication data
A catalogue record for this book is available from the British Library

ISBN 1–84394–062–0

Printed and bound by Alden Group, Oxford

Contents

Appendices:

Introduction

PEOPLE HAVE ALWAYS BEEN INTERESTED in the sun, the moon and the stars. Early in history, perhaps even in prehistory, they did more than just invent myths about them; they got down to serious investigation. Indeed, some early civilizations, notably the Babylonians and the Chinese, evolved a definitely scientific astronomy – and this was long before there was anything scientific about physics or chemistry. Astronomy is the oldest science.

Let us look at the way that people tried to understand what was happening in the sky, dealing first with the sun, then the night sky, the moon and the planets, and finally with early attempts to put things together into a coherent whole.

1

The Sun

SUNRISE, SUNSET

IMAGINE THAT IT IS EARLY IN PREHISTORY. Human beings have developed a sense of beauty. We don't know when that happened, but at some time it did. Sunsets are beautiful and you like to watch them. After a while it strikes you that the sun does not always set in the same place.

We often say 'the sun rises in the east and sets in the west' but this is only roughly true. It rises somewhere on the eastern horizon and sets somewhere on the western horizon. If I watch the sunset from a pier near where I live, I find that in the middle of summer the sun sets directly in front of me, but in the middle of winter it sets well to my left. (Of course, the sun does not really set on the horizon: it is millions of times further away. But it looks as though it does, and I am describing what the eye sees.)

Anyone who watches the sunset regularly will see it move a little each day from furthest left to furthest right and back again. This cycle keeps repeating, and the sun comes back to the same left-most and right-most positions each time.

If you get up early and watch the sun rise you will find a similar movement along the eastern horizon. Sunrise is furthest north when sunset is furthest north and furthest south when sunset is furthest south.

Watching the sunset is a very natural thing to do. My wife and I once lived in Ankara, with a flat plain to the west of us, the horizon being just jagged enough for me to identify the point where the sun set and to follow its day-to-day progress. There is plenty of evidence from anthropologists of primitive peoples watching the position of sunset and sunrise. And there is evidence from archaeology of early people not only watching sunrise and sunset but marking their furthest positions in truly spectacular fashion. The best-known examples are at Stonehenge and Newgrange.

Early Stonehenge, built about 3000 BC, consisted of the circular bank shown in figure 1, and at least the start of the avenue flanked by two straight banks. A stone pillar, usually called the heel-stone, is just tall enough to cut the horizon when seen from the centre of Stonehenge and marks the leftmost, i.e. the most northerly, sunrise. Later, the four station-stones, numbers 91 to 94 in figure 1, were placed to form a rectangle whose short side is parallel to the main axis. Later yet, about 2000 BC, came the circle of huge upright columns and lintels and the U-shaped group of trilithons, made of even larger columns and lintels, whose ruins are so spectacular. The sun rising over the heel-stone on or around the morning of the most northerly sunrise, when seen from the centre, would be framed by two uprights of the circle and the lintel topping them, a spectacle that draws crowds every midsummer and perhaps did much the same when Stonehenge was built. (I am using 'midsummer' in the popular sense; to astronomers this day is the first day of summer.)

Recently a hole has been uncovered beside the heel-stone, and it is possible

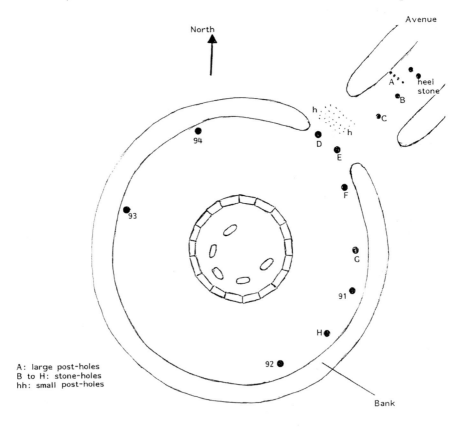

A: large post-holes
B to H: stone-holes
hh: small post-holes

Figure 1

that originally the sunrise appeared in the gap between a stone in this hole and the heel-stone.

Although Stonehenge marks the position of the most northerly sunrise fairly precisely, it does not mark the date of this sunrise with any precision, because the daily movement of sunrise along the horizon at midsummer is quite small, about an eighth of the sun's diameter per day, and the sun seems to rise at the same point for several successive days. This is where the word 'solstice' comes from: *sol* + *stitium* = sun + standstill. Most primitive watchers of the sunrise do in fact say that it stands still for a few days.

There is a slight complication: refraction. This is the bending of the sun's rays as they pass through the atmosphere. When you see the first gleam of the sun at sunrise the sun's rays are reaching you along a curved path. A dead straight line from your eye to the sun would not clear the horizon, and the sun is actually below the horizon, though it seems to be above. Refraction can make the sun appear to be higher than it actually is by a distance equal to its diameter. Because the sun rises and sets obliquely, not vertically, this will affect the position of sunrise or sunset. The exact amount of the refraction depends on the temperature and humidity of the atmosphere, and can vary from one day to the next.

Although the sun appears just above the heel-stone at the solstice today, and even further above when Stonehenge was first built, that is because the heel-stone is now leaning towards the centre of Stonehenge. If it were restored to its upright position it would cover the sun and its shadow would reach the centre of Stonehenge. Terrance Meaden has suggested that this is deliberate. A stone miscalled the altar stone, now fallen, was originally upright at the centre. Meaden suggested that it was a 'goddess stone', that the heel-stone represented a god, and that the shadow-play represented the union of god and goddess.

Stonehenge may also have marked midwinter sunrise. In figure 1, G and H mark holes that might have held stones. If so, sight-lines from 94 to G and 93 to H would mark midwinter sunrise. If you or I were to build a stonehenge we would not mark the two extreme sunrises in such different ways. We would probably place a stone like the heel-stone to the south-east, perhaps with a second entrance and avenue there. Possibly Stonehenge was originally built to mark midsummer sunrise, and the midwinter marking added later. People may not have been around much in midwinter. Salisbury Plain is pretty bleak then.

The most southerly sunrise is marked in an entirely different way at

Newgrange in Ireland. Here an earthen mound, built about 2500 BC, about 80 metres across, contains a long straight passageway that is in just the right direction for sunlight to shine through an opening above the doorway along the passageway at the most southerly sunrise.

It is not only the most northerly and southerly positions of sunrise and sunset that people watched. People who live near a well-marked horizon can use the positions between them as a calendar. There is an example of this at the Hopi village of Sihmapovi (in the southwestern USA), which lies atop a hill and has a well-marked eastern horizon as shown in figure 2. Features on the horizon mark the dates for planting various crops and for holding annual ceremonies.

The Incas, too, used the rising and the setting of the sun to mark important dates. For example, on the skyline east of their capital Cuzco they erected four pillars. When the sunrise reached the first pillar it was time to sow in the mountains above Cuzco, when the sunrise reached the second pillar it was time to sow in the fields around Cuzco, and when the sun rose halfway between the second and third pillars it was time to sow in the valleys below Cuzco.

The astronomers of early civilizations, such as the Babylonian, Greek, Chinese or Indian, did not place much emphasis on the position of sunset on the horizon; (Nor do astronomers today. But craftsmen who install window awnings do, for practical reasons.) But, oddly enough, Galileo had one of his characters mention it in his *Dialogue on the two Chief World Systems.* Salviati said that he observed the sun set behind a rock on the mountains about 60 miles away, leaving a small streak whose width was less than a hundredth of the sun's diameter. The next evening it left a noticeably smaller streak, showing that it had begun to recede.

The eastern horizon seen from Sihmapovi (based on a native drawing)

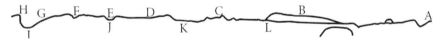

From winter to summer	From summer to winter
A winter solstice ceremony	H summer solstice ceremony
B work in the fields begins	I the last date for planting corn
C onions, chile and early corn planted	J early corn is ripe
D melons and squashes planted	K flute dance
E more corn planted	L the main harvest
F beans and the main crop of corn planted	
G late planting in summer soil	**Figure 2**

The various features have Hopi names. For example, depression F is *walcahoya*, and the peak just to the left of A is *sotapi*. The winter solstice ceremony is *tawaki*; the summer solstice ceremony is *lohalin*.

Alexander Thom has suggested an ingenious way to overcome the difficulty caused by the very slow change of sunset position at the time of the solstice. Find a peak on the horizon whose western edge is just slightly steeper than the path of the setting sun. Station a row of helpers shoulder-to-shoulder facing the peak. As the sun sets, each helper raises a hand when the sun appears from behind the peak. The last helper to raise a hand and the first not to do so will of course be side-by-side, and a line from the point between them to the western edge of the peak gives the direction of sunset very precisely. Do this each day, starting a few days before the solstice. Unfortunately, although this overcomes the difficulty caused by the slow movement of sunset position, it does not overcome the difficulty caused by a possible day-to-day change in refraction.

Nowadays crowds throng Stonehenge on midsummer day, but the spectacle is just as striking the day before or the day after. The builders of Stonehenge might for all we know have had a three- or four-day festival at this time of year. This festival, if there was one, might or might not have been religious – we know nothing of this people's religion.

You will notice another cycle tying in with the cyclic movement of sunrise. The sunrise is furthest left when nights are long and the weather is cold; it is furthest right when nights are short and the weather is warm. You see much the same whether you are in North America, Great Britain, the Middle East or China. (In Australia, though, right and left would be interchanged.)

Imagine that early observers have just noticed this tie-in. What does it mean? What if, one midwinter, the sunrise did not change direction? Would winter go on for ever and summer never come? We don't know whether early people did wonder in this way, but we do know that the Zulus said that when the winter sun began its return it was going to fetch the summer. And the Pueblo tribes in the south-west USA had special 'sun-watchers' whose task was to fix the date of important rites at the winter solstice. It seems highly likely that these rites were originally intended to make the sun return, just as a rain-dance is intended to bring rain.

The movement of sunrise or sunset from one extreme position to the other and back always takes the same length of time. We cannot know whether prehistoric people gave a name to this period – the year – but all early civilizations did.

One more phenomenon ties in with this cycle. In summer the midday sun is higher in the sky than in winter. That is why summer is hot: the sun is beating down more vertically. At midday the sun is always in the same direction from you – south (at least if you are in North America etc. In Australia it is north).

It is clear what is happening. When the sun is high in the sky in summer it sweeps out a bigger path as it rises, climbs across the sky to a point high in the south and sets, than it does in winter, when it climbs only to a point low in the southern sky. It therefore has to rise and set further round the horizon (from south) in summer than in winter.

The size of the sweep along the horizon from the most northerly to the most southerly sunrise (or sunset) and back depends on the place where the observations are made. Someone in Scotland would find a bigger sweep than someone in southern England.

Some early people might have noticed the variations in the height of the midday sun and used it to create a display. At the top of a steep isolated hill called Fajada Butte, in Chaco Canyon in the southwestern USA, are three thin stone slabs so situated that at midsummer midday the sun shining through one of the chinks between them throws a thin vertical line of sunlight, sometimes called a 'sun dagger', onto the face of the rock behind them. The slabs are not quite vertical, and as the sun moves across the sky the dagger moves downwards. The Anasazi, who lived in the canyon around AD 1000, carved a spiral on the face of the rock in such a position that at midsummer the dagger passes through the centre of the spiral. In midwinter the sun shines at midday through both the chinks between the three slabs, and the two sun daggers so formed neatly frame the spiral.

There is another example of shadow-play at the Mayan site of Chichén Itzá in eastern Mexico, midway between midsummer and midwinter.

The tower of Kukulcan is made up of nine square platforms, each smaller than the one on which it rests. Down the middle of each face is a staircase flanked by a low wall, and on each side of the bottom step of the staircase on the north face is a sculptured head of the bird-snake Kukulcan, more familiar perhaps under its Aztec name of Quetzalcoatl. Figure 3 is a free-hand sketch.

Around the middle of spring or autumn the setting sun casts a shadow of the stepped northwest edge of the tower onto the wall of the staircase on the north face, leaving triangles of light on the wall, which imaginative observers see as the body of a diamond-backed rattlesnake, ending at the sculptured head at the foot of the staircase. The spectacle appears every day for several weeks and is at its best about March 25th. Nobody knows whether the Mayas deliberately oriented the tower to give the effect, or even if they noticed the shadow-play at all. Archaeologists have been investigating the site since about 1850 but nobody noticed it before Laura Gilpin published

Figure 3: The Tower of Kukulcan

a photograph, taken in late February, 1946, in her book *The Temples of Yucatan*. (She did not mention a snake; her photograph was simply called *Sunshine and Shadow on the North Balustrade*.)

THE YEAR

THE CYCLE OF MOVEMENTS of sunrise and sunset along the horizon always seems to take the same length of time. How long is this cycle? In other words, how many days are there in a year?

To very early people the year would not be quite the same as it is to us. To them the year would be the period from the day of one summer solstice to the next or from the day of one winter solstice to the next. This year is a whole number of days. But on the modern understanding of the year (and not all that modern – the ancient Babylonians, Chinese and Greeks understood it) the year is not a whole number of days, as we shall see.

It is not possible to pinpoint the exact day on which sunrise or sunset is at its extreme position, and even after instruments for measuring the height of the sun at midday were invented it was not easy to find the exact day on which this height was greatest or least because at the time of the solstice the height changed so little from one day to the next. In spite of this, people did find that the number of days in the primitive year is 365. The Mayas and the Egyptians both knew this. How can we tell? They both had calendars in which the calendar year was 365 days, and there is no other reason for choosing this particular number.

A very early astronomer wants to count the number of days in a year. However, he (all early astronomers that we know of were male) cannot find the day of the solstice exactly. After a little thought he has a bright idea: he counts the number of days between solstices several years apart. If he has the patience to count the days between solstices twenty years apart, and if each solstice is out by at most two days then even if, by bad luck, one solstice is too early and the other too late, the count is not more than four days out. When he divides the total by 20 to find the length of one year, the result will be out by one-fifth of a day at most, and so should be correct to the nearest whole day.

He does this, and gets a surprising result. The year does not work out to be a whole number of days, but close to 365¼ days. There is a hint in one early Chinese source that the Chinese might have thought that three 365-day years were regularly followed by one 366-day year. But they soon gave up this idea (if they in fact ever thought it) and assumed that every year is the same length. So the year is not a whole number of days, and it must be something more subtle than the number of days from one summer (or winter) solstice to the next.

Because the year is not exactly 365 days, the first day of the Egyptian or the Mayan calendar drifted through the seasons as the centuries passed. The first day of the Egyptian year was a summer day in 1350 BC, the era of Tutankhamun; eight hundred years earlier it was a winter day. Between the building of the pyramids and the reign of Tutankhamun enough time elapsed for the Egyptian calendar to drift once-and-a-bit round the seasons. The first day of the Mayan calendar was early summer in AD 300 when Mayan civilization began to flourish, and early winter in AD 1000 when that civilization was coming to an end. The popular idea that the Mayas had a calendar more accurate than ours is totally false.

The 365-day calendar year is sometimes called a wandering year. Through a mistranslation of *vagus*, the Latin for 'wandering', this year is sometimes called a vague year, but there is nothing vague about it.

To see the reason for the odd fraction of a day in the year we need to be more precise about the solstice, and in order to do this I must explain some technical terms.

CIRCLES IN THE SKY

NOWADAYS WE THINK of the earth as spinning on its axis, making one rotation each day, while the stars remain still. Then relative to the earth the sky and everything in it spins about the same axis in the opposite direction. Most earlier astronomers thought of the earth as still, while the sky rotated. (Exceptions: a few Greeks like Aristarchus and at least one Indian, Aryabhata.)

If the sky rotates, the daily paths of the sun in summer, mid-season, and winter are circles with centres on the axis around which they rotate.

Of course, if the distance of the sun from the earth varies in the course of a day the paths will not be circles, but the ancients had no reason to believe that it varies. True, the setting sun looks larger than the sun at midday, but this is an optical illusion. You can test this for yourself. Find a coin of just the right size to cover the sun's disc precisely when held at arm's length at midday. The same coin will cover the sun precisely as it sets. (Make sure that you hold the coin at the same distance from your eye each time.)

A point N on the northern part of the axis of rotation is called the north celestial pole, and a point S on the southern part of the axis is the south celestial pole.

If P and Q are points in the sky, the *angular distance* between them is the angle between the line from you to P and the line from you to Q. (Astronomers use the word 'distance' to apply to angles as well as lengths.) The angular distance between a point and the north celestial pole is the *north polar distance, npd,* of the point. The npd is an important concept in astronomy, and I will be referring to it often.

The *elevation* of a point is its angular distance above the horizon.

The *azimuth* of a point is its angular distance from north.

SOLSTICES

THE FACT THAT THE ELEVATION of the sun at midday is greater in summer than in winter means that its daily path in summer is further north in the northern hemisphere than in winter. This path moves steadily from its northernmost position to its southernmost position and back; the actual path of the sun, relative to the earth, is a tightly-wound spiral.

The precise instant when the sun is at its northernmost position is the northern hemisphere's summer solstice; its southernmost position gives the winter solstice. The solstices can occur at any time of day. It is because they do not occur a whole number of days apart that the year does not consist of a whole number of days.

A FLAT EARTH AND SKY?

SOME EARLY CHINESE astronomers did not believe the system that I have been describing. In their theory the sun revolves in horizontal circles, called *heng*, round the celestial pole. Rising and setting were explained as optical illusions: when the sun appears to set it is simply going beyond the range of human vision. There was no explanation of why the sun does not appear to grow smaller as it gets further away.

There are seven equally-spaced *heng*. The radius of the smallest is half the radius of the largest. At the summer solstice the sun is in the smallest *heng*. One-twelfth of a year later it is in the next larger *heng* and so on until, half a year later, at the winter solstice, it is in the largest *heng*. Evidently this theory assumed that the two solstices divide the year exactly in half. One-twelfth of a year later the sun is in the second-largest *heng* and so on. A year is exactly 365¼ days.

Figures for the sizes of the summer and winter *hengs* were calculated from observations at Zhou, which was just inside the smallest *heng*. The sun in the summer *heng* stays within the range of Zhou longer than in winter (the range of sunlight is the same as the range of human vision); that is why days are longer in summer than in winter. Halfway between the solstices the *yin* and the *yang* are equally balanced, night being *yin* and day being *yang*.

MORE ABOUT THE YEAR

THE YEAR IS THE LENGTH of time from one summer solstice to the next, or from one winter solstice to the next. Is this always the same? No: it varies by up to twenty minutes, as you can check by looking up the times of recent solstices in an almanac. Early astronomers took it for granted that all years were equally long. Exception: the Greek astronomer Hipparchus, about 130 BC. He investigated equinoxes, an equinox being an instant when the sun's daily path is halfway between its extreme positions. Each year there will be an equinox in the spring and one in the autumn. The time from one spring equinox to the next, or from one autumn equinox to the next, is also a year.

Hipparchus cautiously concluded that there was not enough evidence to show that the length of the year varies, whether measured from solstice to solstice or equinox to equinox. This is not surprising, as he quoted the times of the equinoxes only to the nearest quarter of a day; they were listed as dawn, midday, evening or midnight. But even the Chinese, who by the thirteenth century AD could find solstices correct to the nearest hundredth of a day, did not discover the year-to-year variation.

Not only does the length of the year vary from year to year, but according to modern theories the average length of the year changes as the centuries pass, though only very little: it decreases by about half a second per century.

This is not the only way to find the length of the year. An indirect way is to find the number of days in a month and the number of months in a year (a month is the time from one full moon to the next) and multiply the two together. The Chinese used this method for at least one of their early calculations. It is not as silly as it seems at first blush. All early civilizations had an estimate for the length of the month, needed for predicting the dates of new moon and full moon, which was important in the days before street-lighting. And they had estimates for the number of months in a year, needed for setting up a calendar. So all the data were to hand.

From very early times people have tried to estimate the length of the year. Here are some results.

- Chinese, about 500 BC, 8½ minutes too long
- Hipparchus, about 130 BC, 6¼ minutes too long
- Babylonian tablet (between 135 and 65 BC), 5 minutes too long
- Da ming almanac (AD 462), 45 seconds too long
- Tong tian almanac (AD 1199), 21 seconds too long
- Ulugh Beg (AD 1410), 27 seconds too long

The early Chinese estimate was from solstices in 655 and 522 BC, quoted to the nearest day. It was not until much later that anyone could improve on the Chinese estimate of AD 1199. Tycho Brahe, about AD 1580, had an estimate 3 seconds too short.

Modern astronomers have determined the average length of the year very precisely. The nineteenth-century Astronomer Royal, George Airy, once wrote 'I have computed the length of the year: it is 365 days, 5 hours, 48 minutes, 46.05440 seconds. I am sorry to be unable to give you a greater number of decimals.' He did not explain how he determined it so precisely. Nor, in fact, do astronomers ever explain exactly what they mean by the average length of the year. (The average between two given dates is clear enough: the time-interval divided by the number of years. But this will vary slightly according to which two dates are chosen.)

Hipparchus's method was explained by the later Greek astronomer-encyclopaedist Klaudios Ptolemaios, usually called Ptolemy. (Not, of course, one of the pharaohs of that name.) Ptolemy's astronomical encyclopedia, the *Syntaxis* (or, based on the name given to it later by the Arabs, the *Almagest*) is an extensive work of thirteen volumes, written about AD 150, which contains most of what we know about Greek astronomy.

Ptolemy explained that Hipparchus found his estimate by comparing a summer solstice with one observed by Aristarchus 145 years earlier. Ptolemy also explained how he himself found the length of the year. He compared an autumn equinox with one observed by Hipparchus 285 years earlier, and got exactly the same result as Hipparchus. This is shocking. Ptolemy couldn't improve on Hipparchus even though he lived some 300 years later. In fact, the equinox that Ptolemy said that he used actually occurred more than a day earlier than the time that he cited. He made similar calculations with spring equinoxes and summer solstices and got exactly the same wrong result each time. Obviously Ptolemy used Hipparchus's result to calculate the times of the equinoxes and solstices that he said he used, and cited the times that he calculated, pretending that he had observed them.

The Arabic astronomer al-Battani, about AD 900, was a victim of Ptolemy's fraud. He used one of Ptolemy's equinoxes. If Ptolemy had put his equinox on the right day, al-Battani's estimate would have been out by half a minute; in fact it was out by 2½ minutes. But for Ptolemy's fraud, al-Battani would have been about as accurate as the Chinese at around the same date.

FINDING NORTH AND SOUTH

BY WATCHING SUNRISE and sunset we might possibly be able to find the *day* on which a solstice occurs, but we certainly won't be able to find the *time* of the solstice. Nor will the height of the midday sun give us the time of the solstice. We need better methods. It turns out that most of these methods depend on an accurate north-to-south direction. Let us see how we could find this.

One way to find north is to set up a vertical rod, using plumb-lines to make sure that it is vertical, on a flat horizontal base, using grooves filled with water to ensure that it is accurately horizontal. As the sun rises in the sky, the shadow of the rod grows shorter, and as the sun moves towards the west the shadow turns. When the shadow is shortest it is pointing north. A rod used in this way is called a *gnomon.*

It is not easy to tell precisely when the shadow is shortest, but we can inscribe a circle on the base a little longer than the shortest shadow, and mark the two points where the tip of the shadow is on the circle. The line joining them will run east-to-west, and the point halfway between them will be due north of the foot of the rod. This method was used by Vedic astronomers in India, perhaps about 1000 BC.

This method is not very precise, but once we know approximately where north is, we can find it more accurately at night.

Hang a vertical string as near to the north of your viewing-point as you can. By watching the stars turn you can see roughly where the celestial pole is. Set up a thin horizontal rod across the string and watch a bright star near the pole. The star will cross the horizontal rod twice, once on the way up and once on the way down. If the string is in the right position it will be exactly halfway between the points where the star crosses the rod. If it isn't, move it over a bit and check on the next night to see if it is now right. You will soon have it accurately north of your viewing-position.

MEASURING ELEVATION

THE NEXT STEP is to find accurately the elevation of the sun at midday. We run an accurately-levelled scale along the ground due north from the foot of a gnomon. When the shadow of the gnomon falls on the scale it is midday and time to read the length of the shadow. The snag is that the sun is not a point source of light but a sizeable body. In figure 4 the stretch AC is shielded from the sun and is in full shadow. Between C and D the shadow lightens, and beyond D the scale is in full sunlight. The eye is not able to judge the middle of DC but judges the shadow to end close to C. You can check this for yourself. At latitude 50°, midsummer noon, with a gnomon 1.6 metres high, the length of CD is about 18 millimetres. But the fuzzy tip of the shadow that you will see is only one or two millimetres. So we are not measuring the elevation of the centre of the sun; we are measuring the elevation of its top edge. Our measurement is too big by half the diameter of the sun; that is, by about a quarter of a degree.

So let us fix a horizontal rod at the top of the gnomon, at right angles to the scale. If the rod is just thick enough its shadow will have a dark streak down the middle, which will give the elevation of the centre of the sun.

The early Greeks did not think of this and indeed there is evidence that Eratosthenes, who lived about 200 BC, made the quarter-degree error that I have been describing. (Details later, in the section on the size of the earth.)

The Chinese did use a horizontal rod, and they forked the top of the gnomon to hold it, sometimes carving the two tines of the fork into ornamental dragons. The standard Chinese gnomon throughout most of their history was 80 inches high. (The Chinese inch – *cun* in Chinese – was about 25 millimetres.)

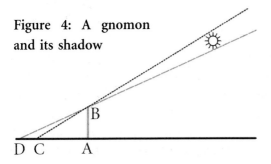

Figure 4: A gnomon and its shadow

D C   A   B

Everyone knows that larger instruments give greater precision. One Arab astronomer (perhaps with his tongue in his cheek) said that if he could get enough funding to build an instrument reaching from the pyramids to Mount Muqattam he would do so.

What stops a gnomon from becoming really big is the indistinctness of the shadow. The Chinese overcame this snag in a most ingenious way. They used a copper plate pierced by a hole 'as big as a grain of rice'. They held it (or fixed it in a framework) a little way above the scale in such a position that the shadow of the cross-bar fell on the hole. Then the sunlight shining through the hole forms a spot of light on the scale, and across this small circle of light is a beautifully sharp image of the cross-bar. You can try it yourself; a hole punched in a postcard will do. The sharpness of the image is quite striking. If necessary, move the postcard up or down the scale until the image of the cross-bar divides the circle of light exactly in half, and read off its position on the scale.

This device enabled Guo Shoujing, about AD 1300, to use a gnomon five times the standard size. The measurements that he made with it at Beijing are preserved in the annals of the Yuan dynasty. This gnomon has disappeared but at Dengfeng there is a brick tower about 9 metres high with a scale for measuring shadows running due north from the middle of its north face. A horizontal rod 400 Chinese inches above the scale (the height of Guo's gnomon) would be conveniently waist-high for anyone working on the top of the tower.

Another instrument is a vertical north-to-south wall with a circular scale marked on its eastern face. A horizontal rod juts out from the centre of the scale. The instant when the shadow fades is midday and the reading of the last visible shadow gives the elevation of the sun then. We do not need the whole of the circular scale; a quarter will do, in which case we have a wall-quadrant. (Figure 5.)

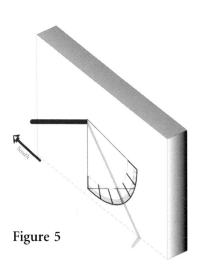

Figure 5

A better instrument is shown in figure 6. It is aligned north-to-south. The shadow of the rod falls along the centre of the scale at midday, and the shadow of the horizontal cross-bar, which is at the centre of the circle of which the scale forms part, gives the elevation of the sun then. This could be built against a wall, with the horizontal rod jutting out from the wall instead of being carried by the vertical pole. A hollow sighting-tube could be pivoted on the rod and turned so that the sun shines through it onto the scale. Alternatively, the rod could carry a plate with a hole through which the sun would shine at midday, casting a splash of light on the scale. The Arabs used a large instrument of this sort. Its radius was about 20 metres. The bright patch would be fuzzy, but by placing a ring fitted with cross-wires on it they could find the centre fairly accurately.

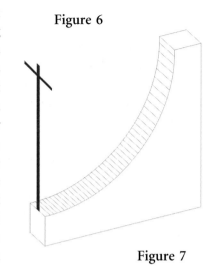

Figure 6

The largest and consequently the most precise instrument of this type that we know of is the huge quadrant (with a radius of just over forty metres) built by Ulugh Beg at Samarkand a little after AD 1400. It was contained in a circular building as shown in figure 7. The quadrant was double, as shown in figure 8, and an observer could sit on the steps between its two parts, which were furnished with grooves a degree apart. A sighting device like the one shown in figure 9 could be set down accurately by fitting two ridges on its underside into two successive grooves. To read off fractions of a degree the peep-hole shown could be slid along the slot. The observer looked through the peep-hole towards cross-wires at A in figure 7, the centre of the circle of which the quadrant forms part. Because it does not depend on shadows this instrument has no snags caused by fuzziness.

Figure 7

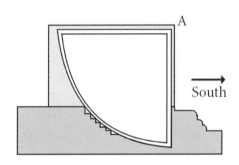

South

Another instrument is a grad-uated disc set on a post and fitted with a sighting-rod, as shown in figure 10. If the post is vertical as

Figure 8

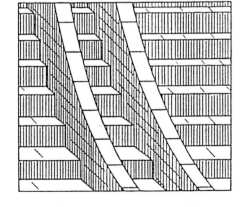

shown the instrument measures elevation. A graduated horizontal circle round the middle enables it to measure azimuths. If the post points towards

Figure 9: Ulugh Beg's sighting device

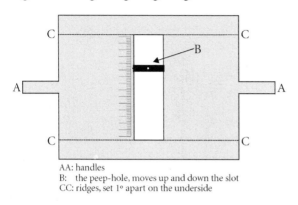

AA: handles
B: the peep-hole, moves up and down the slot
CC: ridges, set 1° apart on the underside

the north celestial pole instead of being vertical, the instrument measures npds and angular distances round the equator. Figure 11 shows a large and comparatively late instrument of this type (date about AD 1590).

To set such an instrument up we need to find the elevation of the pole. To do this we measure the greatest and least elevations of a star near the pole (these are its elevations when it is due north of the observer) and take the elevation halfway between them. For example, we could use the method described on page 3 for finding north accurately. After adjusting the vertical string correctly we adjust the horizontal rod until it is halfway between the points where the star crosses the string. The elevation of the point where the rod crosses the string is the elevation of the pole.

A small portable version of the instrument shown in figure 10 can be made by fitting a suspension-ring at the top, from which it can hang vertically, instead of fixing it to a stand. Less precise – more convenient.

To sight a star, hold the instrument at eye-level. To sight the sun, hold it at waist-level and turn it until the sun shines along the sighting-tube or, if using a rod fitted with sights, until the shadow of the foresight falls on the backsight. Having each sight pierced by a small hole through which you can see the star or through which the sun can shine makes the instrument as precise as can be expected from a portable instrument. Many medieval astrolabes were fitted with sighting-rods, a graduated

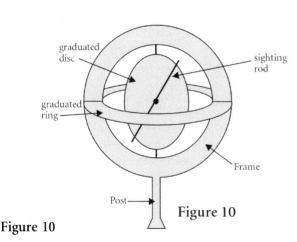

graduated disc

sighting rod

graduated ring

Frame

Post

Figure 10

Figure 10

rim, and a suspension ring, to be used like this. (The astrolabe will be described later.)

These instruments can be used to find the elevations of stars. So can the gnomon. An early Chinese text explains that this is done by attaching a string to the top of the gnomon and pulling it taut in such a way that it is aligned on the star whose elevation is being measured. The point where it reaches the ground is noted, and the distance of this point from the foot of the gnomon gives the elevation of the star.

This method seems highly impractical at first blush, but here is how it could work. Fix a small ring, to be used as a backsight, on a tripod. I used a camera tripod; the Chinese could have used three bamboo sticks. Move the tripod around until the tip of the gnomon, viewed through the ring, just covers the star. Thread the string through the ring and pull it taut, being careful not to move the ring. Slide your finger and thumb down the string, still very careful not to move the ring, until they reach the ground.

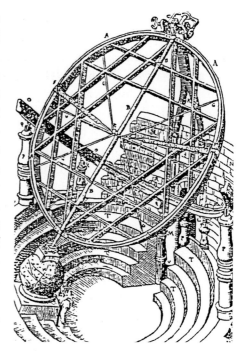

Figure 11: Armilla from Stjerneborg

MORE ON THE EARLY CHINESE THEORY

I CAN NOW EXPLAIN how the Chinese determined the figures in their flat-earth theory. They had noticed that the shadow of a gnomon at midday on the summer solstice was shorter at places further south than at places further north. They had somehow come to believe that for every 1000 *li* further south (a *li* is about half a kilometre) the shadow of a standard gnomon of height 80 (Chinese) inches shortened by 1 inch. They believed that this is true also at the winter solstice and in fact that it holds in general.

This belief is wrong in several ways. First, the change is not the same in winter as in summer. Second, it depends on the latitude of the place of observation. Worst of all, the figure is hopelessly wrong. At the latitude of central China a change of 1 inch in the length of the shadow would need a displacement of only about 150 *li* in summer and about 40 *li* in winter.

The most detailed description of the flat-earth theory is in a collection of texts called *Zhou bi*, the gnomon of Zhou, probably compiled by various authors in the Han dynasty, which lasted roughly from 200 BC to AD 200, but possibly based on earlier observations and musings. (The Chinese character for Zhou is not only a place name but also has various meanings including 'circumference' and the title *Zhou bi* has been translated in various ways.)

The shadow of a standard gnomon at midsummer noon at Zhou is 16 inches. This means, on the Zhou bi theory, that 16,000 *li* south of Zhou the shadow will have zero length, so that the sun is, at midsummer noon, directly over this point. Not only that but the L-shaped figure formed by the shadow and the gnomon has the same proportions as the L-shaped figure formed by the line from the gnomon to the point Q vertically below the sun and the vertical line from Q to the sun. For each inch in the shadow there are 1,000 *li* in the distance from the

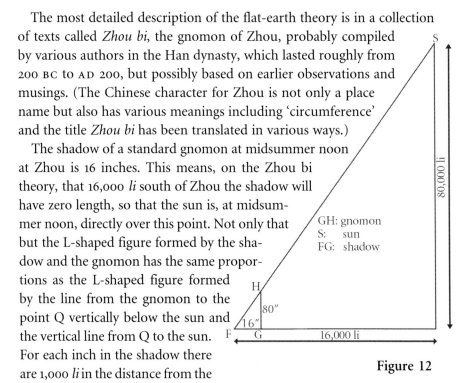

Figure 12

gnomon to Q, so for each inch in the gnomon there are 1,000 *li* in the vertical line from Q to the sun. There are 80 inches in the gnomon, so the sun is 80,000 *li* above the earth. (Figure 12 shows this.)

The shadow at midwinter noon is 135 inches, so by the same reasoning the sun then is 135,000 *li* south of Zhou and is again 80,000 *li* above the earth. (The shadow lengths quoted are reasonable for the latitude of central China.)

Elementary geometry tells us that if the sun is always 80,000 *li* above a flat earth the shadow of an 80-inch gnomon will indeed change by one inch for every thousand *li* change in the position of the sun.

To return to the *Zhou bi*: the north celestial pole is found by the string method to be 103,000 *li* north of Zhou. We do not know which star was used as pole star (*ji xing* in Chinese): our Polaris was not near the pole in those days.

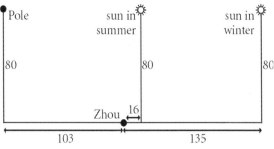

A side view of the universe according to the *Zhou bi* distances are in thousands of *li*

Figure 13

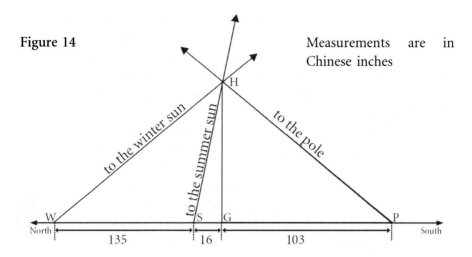

Figure 14

Measurements are in Chinese inches

The dimensions imply a very large earth, stretching over 100,000 kilometres south of the north pole. For all we know the Chinese might not have been interested in the size of the earth, but simply assumed that it went on for ever. (Figure 13 shows this.)

The figure quoted for the pole is highly suspicious. The distance of the end of the string from the foot of the gnomon should have been 114 inches, not 103 inches. In figure 14, GH is the gnomon, WH and SH sight the sun at midday on the winter and summer solstices respectively, and PH sights the pole. WP = 238 inches and SP = 119 inches, so the sun is exactly twice as far from the pole in winter as it is in summer. It looks as though someone wanted this neat result and fudged the measurement to get it.

FINDING THE SOLSTICE PRECISELY

THE CHINESE gave a good description of how they used the gnomon to find solstices accurately. The method was invented by Zu Chongzhi about AD 450.

The time of a winter solstice is an instant when the sun's npd is greatest. The gnomon keeps track of the npd at midday: the greater the npd the longer the shadow. The npd increases steadily until the solstice and then decreases, so the question is: how, from measurements made only at noon, can we find the instant when the npd is greatest?

We start by measuring the shadow a few days before the solstice. Let us suppose that it is 160 inches on the 14th of the month. The midday shadow lengthens and then shortens and we note its length on the last day on which it is longer than 160 inches and on the next day. Let us suppose that it is

170 inches on the 22nd and 140 inches on the 23rd. We calculate by proportion the time between midday on the 22nd and midday on the 23rd when
the npd is the same as at noon on the 14th. On the figures just quoted, the
shadow on the 14th differs from the shadow on the 22nd by 10 inches and
from the shadow on the 23rd by 20 inches, giving a ratio of 1 to 2. We
divide the interval between the two noons in this ratio, giving a time
one-third of a day after midday on the 22nd. The solstice is midway between
this time and midday on the 14th, which will be one-sixth of a day after
noon on the 18th.

This method assumes that the npd varies at a constant rate between noons
on the 22nd and 23rd, that the difference between midday values of the
npd is proportional to the difference between the lengths of the corresponding midday shadows, and that the motion of the sun is symmetrical about
the solstice. None of these assumptions is strictly accurate; nevertheless the
method works well. The Chinese were able to find solstices, using this
method and Guo's giant gnomon, correct to the nearest hundredth of a
day.

From at least AD 442 onwards the Chinese were quoting times of solstices
in *ke*, a *ke* being one-hundredth of a day. (This does not necessarily mean that
they were correct to the nearest *ke* in these early days.)

How did the early Greeks find the times of the solstices? We have very
few records of early solstices, but plenty of records of equinoxes. These
were recorded as midnight, morning, noon or evening, and it seems likely
that solstices would be recorded to the same degree of precision – much
less precise than the Chinese but better than merely quoting the day of the
solstice. The Greeks have not left us a description of their method, but it
is not hard to find a fairly obvious method that yields just this degree of
precision. Knowing roughly when the solstice is, record the elevation of the
sun at noon each day, starting a few days before the solstice – in fact, long
enough before for the difference in elevation to be detectable. You hope to
find two days, one before the solstice and one after, when the two elevations
are equal. The solstice is half-way between these two noons. The snag is
that you often won't find two equal elevations.

So you will have to modify the method. Measure the elevation at noon
a few days before the summer solstice. Call this day zero and the elevation
x. Each noon from then on the elevation will be greater until the solstice
has passed, and then it will decrease. Pick out the first day on which the
elevation is less than *x*. The previous day is the last day on which it is
greater than *x*. Suppose that these are days 4 and 5. Assume that the time
when the npd of the sun corresponds to an elevation *x* is the instant halfway

between these two noons. This will be midnight on day 4. The time half-way between this instant and noon on day zero is the time of the solstice; in this case, 2¼ days after noon on day zero, which is the evening of day 2.

Of course, you might find a day after the solstice on which the elevation is *x*, in which case the solstice is halfway between this noon and noon on day zero. This method will always give a result 0, ¼, ½ or ¾ of a day after noon, just as we find in Greek records.

The Arabs quoted the times of solstices quite precisely, but I have not been able to find any description of how they did it.

EQUINOXES

I MENTIONED EARLIER that some Greek astronomers used equinoxes as well as solstices for finding the length of the year. Finding an equinox depends on the fact that the sun's north-to-south movement is symmetrical: its south polar distance at the winter solstice is the same as its npd at the summer solstice so that at a position halfway between them – the equinox – the sun's npd is a right angle.

So we want to find the instant when the sun's npd is a right angle. One instrument that the Greeks used for this purpose was called a *krikos*. It is a large bronze ring set up in a plane at right angles to the pole-to-pole axis. We can tell when the sun is in the plane of the ring (if this happens in the daytime and no clouds are in the way) because then one half casts its shadow on the other half.

Watching this is not like watching a sunset. The setting sun moves fairly quickly towards the horizon, at the rate of one revolution round the earth every 24 hours. Its motion relative to the bronze ring is much slower, being caused by the north-to-south motion of the sun, whose speed at the equinox is less than half a degree per day. If you watch the sun near an equinox you will find that it moves almost parallel to the bronze ring and its distance from the plane of the ring changes very slowly. This means that the observations will take a long time. Part of that time the sun will be near the horizon. But then the observations are seriously affected by refraction, which is strongest when the object being viewed is near the horizon. The change in apparent position caused by changes in refraction can overcome the slow change in the sun's real position and reverse its apparent motion towards or away from the ring. Then the ring may overshadow itself two or three times several hours apart. The Greeks made an observation with such a ring at Alexandria in the spring of 146 BC and reported that the ring overshadowed itself at dawn and again five hours later. This equinox is the only one using a *krikos* whose record survives, and is the only one recorded to closer than a quarter-day precision (except for Ptolemy's fraudulent ones).

Equinoxes reported as at midnight, morning, midday or evening were probably calculated in the same way as solstices, perhaps by using an instrument like the one in figure 6, 7 or 10. For equinoxes the method would work like this: first find the scale-readings at noon on the two solstices. The reading half-way between them is the equinox value: let us call it *x*. Note this value, perhaps even marking it on your scale. Knowing approximately the date of the equinox, take readings each noon, starting a few days before the equinox. Call the day of the first reading day zero. Note the difference between this reading and *x*, and call this difference *y*. You may find that one reading is exactly *x*; if so, the equinox is that noon. If not, you might find a reading after the equinox differing from *x* by precisely *y*; if so, the equinox is halfway between that noon and noon on day zero. Failing this, note the first day after the equinox when the difference is greater than *y*. The day before will be the last day on which the difference is less than *y*. Take the instant halfway between these two noons to be the instant when the difference is theoretically *y*. The time halfway between this instant and noon on day zero is the time of the equinox.

THE PATH OF THE SUN

TO SEE HOW early astronomers pictured the movement of the sun we have to look at the stars.

Even without clocks it is not hard to judge the instant of midnight, halfway between sunset and sunrise. If we look at the stars at successive midnights we find that they are not always in the same position. Figure 15 shows the position of one fairly recognizable constellation and the pole star at midnight on one day, a month later, and two months later. (You may recognize the constellation as the Big Dipper, with its two 'pointers'.) The diagrams show only one constellation (for clarity), but the whole skyful of stars rotates in the same way.

Midnight to midnight is the time that the sun takes to make a complete revolution round the earth, so the sky is rotating, relative to the earth, faster than the sun. The midnight sky makes a complete revolution in just a year.

The sun is slipping backwards against the starry background – as the sky rotates westward at one revolution per day the sun slips eastward relative to the stars at a rate of one revolution per year. A Chinese writer likened

Looking North

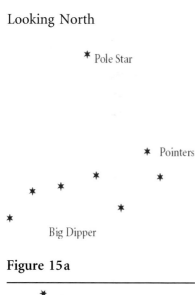

Figure 15a

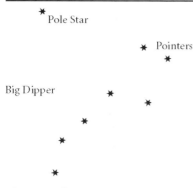

Figure 15b

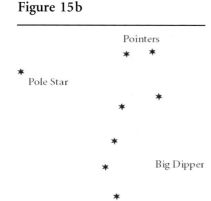

Figure 15c

Figure 15 The Big Dipper at three different times

the sun to an ant crawling on a millstone, being carried round by the millstone much faster than it can crawl in the opposite direction.

At the same time the sun is moving from north to south and back each year, so the idea arose quite naturally that the sun moves, relative to the starry background, in a slanting circle.

Imagine in the sky a large circle whose centre is the earth, fixed relative to the stars. The sun moves round this circle, which we call the sun's *orbit*. The orbit is at an angle to the pole-to-pole axis, i.e. it is slanting, and the sun is at the northernmost point of the orbit in the (northern hemisphere's) midsummer, and the southernmost point in midwinter. Meanwhile, the orbit itself is rotating round the pole-to-pole axis at the same rate as the stars.

The earliest clear picture of this motion was presented by the Greek astronomer and mathematician Eudoxus, between 400 and 300 BC. He imagined a thin transparent hollow sphere rotating round the pole-to-pole axis once a day. Inside it, a second sphere rotates once a year round an axis, inclined to the pole-to-pole axis, carried by the first sphere. A model of the system is shown in figure 16 (in which the transparent spheres are shown shaded, for clarity).

S is the first sphere, AB is the pole-to-pole axis, and a small motor at B drives S. S carries pivots at P and Q which fit into holes in the inner sphere T. A small motor at Q drives T.

A point on the inner sphere equally

far from P and Q represents the sun. As the inner sphere rotates, this point moves around the circle that consists of all the points on the sphere equally far from P and Q. (If the sphere were the earth and P and Q the poles, this circle would be the equator.) This circle is the sun's orbit, and as the outer sphere rotates the orbit rotates while the sun moves slowly round it.

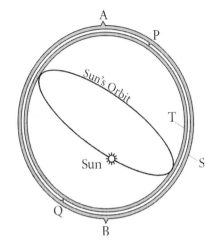

Figure 16: Eudoxus' model for the motion of the sun

Unfortunately, Eudoxus incorporated a third sphere which made the sun deviate from the path I have just described. We do not know why. Perhaps he thought that the sun did not reach the same north polar distance every solstice. This could be shown by the sun not rising (or setting) at exactly the same point of the horizon every summer (or winter) solstice. A difference between the effects of refraction at two solstices could cause this. We have no direct evidence that the Greeks observed sunrise or sunset at the solstices, but they might have been in touch with people who did.

The Babylonians, in tablets dated shortly after 700 BC, described the path of the moon in the sky by listing the constellations on its path. This is easy to do if we watch the moon over a period of time. Later, the Babylonians realized that the centre-line of the belt covered by these constellations was the path of the sun, and by 300 BC they had divided this path into twelve equal sections; they named each section after a constellation that appears to be in it. The Greeks took over this arrangement, translating some of the names and altering others, and this gives us the signs of the zodiac. Our modern names are translations of the Greek ones. (Sometimes we use the translation into Latin: Aries, Taurus etc.) The signs (the Babylonian are in the shaded area) are:

workman	star	twins	?	lion	furrow
ram	bull	twins	crab	lion	virgin

scales	scorpion	[a god]	goat-fish	?	tails
scales	scorpion	archer	he-goat	waterman	fish

A mnemonic for remembering the order of the signs is:

The ram, the bull, the heavenly twins,
next the crab, the lion shines
the virgin and the scales
the scorpion, archer and he-goat,
the man who bears the watering-pot
the fish with glittering tails.*

The Babylonians divided each of the twelve signs into thirty equal parts, getting a small unit, which they called an *ush*. There are 360 *ush* to a complete circle, so an *ush* is in fact a degree. Did the Babylonians in some mysterious way foresee the modern unit? No. They were not using our unit; we are using theirs. The Greeks took over the *ush* and we took it over from the Greeks.

This is far from being the only way to measure angles. Sailors use *points*. There are 32 points in a circle; one point is the angle from north to north-northeast and by north. A yacht sailing north-east in a north wind is 'four points from the wind'. Chinese astronomers divided the circle into 365¼ *du*. I translate *du* as (Chinese) degree. To the Chinese one degree is the angular distance covered by the sun in one day. The metric system divides a circle into 400 units called *grads*. Mathematicians use a highly sophisticated unit called the *radian*. (There are 6.283185 ... of them in a circle. I am not pulling your leg.)

THE IRREGULAR SUN

LET US USE our imaginations again. It is way back in history, and astronomers have just reached the stage when they can find the correct day of the solstice, and they can find the length of the year fairly accurately.

You have been pinpointing the winter solstice, and you meet another astronomer, who has been pinpointing the summer solstice. Knowing the date of the last winter solstice you think that you know the date of the previous summer solstice – half a year earlier. You tell the other astronomer the date. He says 'You're wrong. I've found the summer solstice, and it's two days later than you say.' He then calculates the date of the winter solstice, and finds it two days earlier than you did.

After a bit of an argument you admit that his method of finding the solstice is sound, and he admits that yours is. So you come to the only

---

*Today the signs of the zodiac are used only by astrologers, not by astronomers.

possible conclusion: the solstices do not divide the year exactly in half. The sun must move irregularly round its orbit.

In 200 BC it was four days less from midsummer to midwinter than from midwinter to midsummer. The figures change slightly over the centuries; when Chinese astronomy was at its height, about AD 1250, the two intervals were almost equal.

The equinoxes are not halfway between the solstices, so the four seasons (equinox to solstice, to equinox, to solstice, to equinox) are not equally long. The earliest record that we have of this inequality of the seasons is from the Greek astronomers Meton and Euctemon, between 450 and 400 BC. Although Eudoxus was later than these two his model did not allow for this inequality.

The Babylonians had two ways of dealing with the inequality of the seasons. In fact, they had two systems of mathematical astronomy. Historians have somewhat unimaginatively called them system A and system B.

In system A, which was in use from 263 BC (or earlier: we might not have found the earliest tablets) to 4 BC (or later) the sun moves from 27° in 'tails' to 27° in 'furrows' at 30° per month and for the rest of the year at 15/16 of this rate. We don't know whether the Babylonians thought that the sun's speed changed suddenly or whether they thought that the theory was a good enough approximation that was simple enough for their calculations.

In system B, which was in use at least from 251 BC to 68 BC, the sun moved in a more complicated but smoother way. Its speed increased at a constant rate round part of the zodiac and decreased at a constant rate round the rest.

By AD 604 the Chinese had a theory very like system B. By AD 1280 they had developed it into a system that was smoother, more accurate and much more complicated.

Hipparchus dealt with the inequality of the seasons quite differently. Instead of having the sun move at a variable speed round a circle whose centre is the earth, he had it move at constant speed round a circle whose centre is offset from the earth. There is no way by which he could have known that the orbit is a circle – in fact it isn't quite – or that the speed is constant (again, it isn't quite). But it was a Greek philosophical dogma that heavenly motions are regular circular motions: a point moving at constant speed round a fixed circle is moving regularly, and a point moving at constant speed round a circle whose centre is moving regularly is also moving regularly. The dogma probably came either from Plato or from the followers of Pythagoras.

Whatever philosophers may have thought, later Greek astronomers did not take this dogma seriously. Ptolemy in particular violated it. He was criticized for this, not by Greeks as far as we know but, much later, by Arabic astronomers and by Copernicus.

Hipparchus's theory portrayed the sun's motion relative to the earth remarkably accurately, and the geometry needed is much simpler than the arithmetic needed for the Chinese tables.

Hipparchus's theory is shown in figure 17. The centre of the sun's orbit is C. The earth is T (terra). The distance CT is small, about one twenty-fifth of the radius of the orbit (the diagram is not to scale). To be able to calculate the direction of the sun from the earth at any given instant, Hipparchus had to find the ratio of the distance CT to the radius of the orbit, and the direction of C from the earth. These two quantities are called the *parameters* of the theory; they are respectively the *eccentricity* and the direction of *apogee*. The reason for the name apogee is that it is when the sun is in this direction that it is furthest from the earth.

To find the parameters, Hipparchus used a procedure which seems to have been standard with ancient Greek astronomers. (At least, it was used throughout Ptolemy's *Syntaxis*.) From his theory he determined the fewest items of raw data that he needed, and calculated the par-

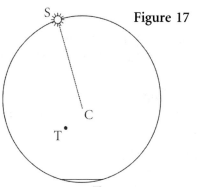

Figure 17

The sun moves at a constant speed around a circle with the centre C, T is the Earth

Hipparchus' theory for the motion of the sun

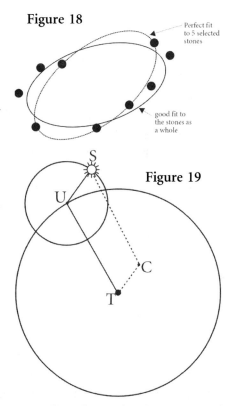

Figure 18

Perfect fit to 5 selected stones

good fit to the stones as a whole

Figure 19

An Indian theory for the motion of the sun

ameters from them. It turns out that the data needed were the length of the year and the lengths of two of the seasons.

The minimum-data principle is as though we were investigating a ring of standing stones left by megalithic builders and had decided in advance that they were set up in an ellipse, but might have moved as time passed. To find the ellipse on which they originally lay we use the geometrical fact that five points are enough to determine an ellipse. We pick the five stones whose positions we think are best preserved and construct the ellipse through them. Modern mathematicians, by contrast, would try to find the ellipse that best fits the stones as a whole. This requires some sophisticated statistical theory. Figure 18 illustrates the two approaches.

Once the parameters are known, together with the position of the sun at one particular instant, for which any accurately-timed solstice will do, we can compute the position of the sun at any desired time. The *Syntaxis* does the calculation for us. One table tells us the position of the sun at the instant; it gives the angle between CS and CN where S is the sun and N is the position where the sun is at the spring equinox, (so N is a fixed point from which the angle is measured). We look this angle up in a second table, which tells us what has to be added to it or subtracted from it to give the direction of the sun from the earth; that is, it gives the angle between SC and ST in figure 17.

Indian astronomers from the fifth century AD onwards had the same theory but described it differently. Imagine a body U rotating round the earth (T) at a rate of one revolution per year in a circle (shown in diagram 19) the same size as the circle in diagram 17. S* is at a distance from U equal to TC in diagram 17, and in a direction parallel to TC. Then S* coincides with S, as the dashed lines make clear. However, not all Indian astronomers had the direction of US* quite fixed. One astronomer had it rotating at a rate of one revolution every nine million years. (No one knows how he obtained this fantastic figure.)

Hipparchus's theory is amazingly effective. It was used by the Arabs and by Europeans up to the time of Kepler (just after AD 1600). Inaccuracies were due to inaccurate parameters rather than a defective theory, and as time passed astronomers found better and better parameters.

HOW FAR AWAY IS THE SUN?

WHEN WE TURN from early attempts to find the direction of the sun at any instant to early attempts to find the distance of the sun from the earth we turn from a story of success to a story of dismal failure. The sun is so far away that measurement is incredibly difficult. The Babylonians and the Mayas did not try to determine the distance of the sun; the Chinese, the Greeks and the Indians did.

I explained the Chinese method on page 19. The Greeks and the Indians used an indirect method: they found the ratio of the distance of the moon from the earth to the distance of the sun from the earth. Although they found the distance of the moon reasonably accurately, they got the ratio badly wrong.

Before the Greeks made any measurements they had surmises. First, they guessed at the size of the sun – since we know how big it looks, its size will tell us its distance and vice versa. Heraclitus (540 to 480 BC) thought that the size is a foot wide (and that each day a new sun is created). He cannot have tested this by placing a disc a foot wide at a distance from his eye that makes it look the same size as the sun. A little later, Anaxagoras thought that the sun is a fiery ball bigger than the Pelopennesos. Earlier than either of these, Anaximander (610 to 547 BC) had some very individual ideas. He thought that the sun is really a tube filled with fire encircling the earth (presumably occupying the sun's orbit). Its diameter is either 27 or 28 times the diameter of the earth. What we see as the sun is a circular hole in the tube, which occasionally closes, causing eclipses. The sun is the same size as the earth. There is a contradiction here: if the sun were as big as the earth and as far away as Anaximander said, it would appear four times as big as it actually does.

The first serious attempt to calculate the distance that has come down to us was made by Aristarchus, just after 300 BC. His method is simple in theory. At exactly half-moon he measured (or guessed) the angle between the line from the earth to the sun and the line from the moon to the sun. He did not have trigonometrical tables, but he found a way to calculate the value that he wanted without them. Unfortunately, he thought that the vital angle was one-thirtieth of a right angle, which made the sun between 18 and 20 times as far away as the moon. In fact, the angle is about one five-hundredth of a right angle, and the sun is 360 times as far away as the moon.

Ptolemy explained a more complicated method, which he attributed to Hipparchus. It depended, among other things, on the diameter of the earth's shadow on the moon, which can be found by studying eclipses. The method is sound in theory but is very sensitive to errors in angles too small to measure accurately, and Ptolemy made the sun 19 times as far away as the moon.

The distance of the sun from the earth varies slightly, but neither Aristarchus nor Ptolemy allowed for this, although Ptolemy could have calculated the ratio of the radius of the sun's orbit to the distance of the sun at the time of observation.

The Indians had an entirely different approach. They assumed that the sun and the moon moved at the same speed round the earth. (So did the planets for that matter.) Aryabhata (about AD 500) had the sun making 4,320,000 revolutions while the moon made 57,753,336, just over 13 times as many. This would make the sun just over 13 times as far away as the moon.

AN IMPORTANT ANGLE

THE ANGLE BETWEEN the plane of the sun's orbit and the plane of the equator is important. It is called the *obliquity of the ecliptic* (because, as explained later, the sun's orbit is called the ecliptic). It is often called simply the *obliquity*. It is half of the difference between the npds of the sun at the two solstices.

The obliquity is also half the angle between the elevations of the sun at midday on the two solstices. People more confident of their measurements of the sun than of the pole would prefer to find the obliquity from these two elevations. The Chinese, with their giant gnomons, found it in this way. This also yields the elevation of the pole: halfway between the two solstice elevations is the elevation of the equator and at right angles to this is the elevation of the pole. This technique is much better than using a gnomon and string.

The Babylonians did not leave any figures for the obliquity. The earliest figures that we have are from the Greeks. We can deduce Hipparchus's estimates from the figures recorded for the length of the longest day at various places, which depends on the obliquity – if the obliquity were zero all days would be equally long. To begin with he used the figure 23°55'. Later he used the more accurate value 23°40'. The correct value in his time was 23°43'.

The Indians used the round number 24°. The early Chinese used 24 Chinese degrees, which equals 23°39'. (A Chinese degree is the average distance that the sun will cover in a day if a year is 365¼ days long. So there are 365¼ of them to a complete circle of 360°.)

The angle between the greatest and least npd of the sun is twice the obliquity. Its value in Ptolemy's time was 47°28', but he said that he always found it to be between 47°40' and 47°45'. He went on to remark that this is 11/83 of a complete circle and agrees with a figure used earlier by Eratosthenes and also by Hipparchus. In fact, there is no evidence that Eratosthenes used this figure and we know that Hipparchus did not. And 11/83 of a circle is a very odd way to describe an angle.

As time passed, astronomers found the obliquity more and more accurately. By AD 900 al-Battani had it correct to within one-hundredth of a degree. By AD 1400 Ulugh Beg had it almost exactly. These accurate figures did not reach Europe. Copernicus had a figure out by one twenty-fifth of a degree.

The obliquity does not remain constant, but the change is very slow: it decreases by about one-hundredth of a degree per century.

HOW LONG IS THE DAY?

ONE IMPORTANT THING that depends on the sun is the length of the day. Astronomers define daytime as the period between sunrise, when the centre of the sun clears a flat horizon, and sunset. This is not the length of daylight because the sky lightens before the sun rises and remains light after it sets. That is why lighting-up time is half an hour after sunset. One Chinese source said quite definitely that astronomical day and night are determined by sunrise and sunset, but civil day and night are determined by light and darkness. It is always light 2½ *ke* before sunrise and it does not become dark until 2½ *ke* after sunset. (A *ke* is one-hundredth of a day, so 2½ *ke* is 36 minutes.)

The Babylonians dealt with the length of the day as follows. The time from sunrise to sunset when the sun is at a certain position in its orbit is the time taken for half of the orbit, starting at the point where the sun is, to rise. In figure 20, A and B are the ends of a sign of the zodiac. The line CB is drawn in the direction in which B moves as the sky turns relative to the earth, and the length of CB shows how far the sky has to turn for AB to rise. This will depend on the angle between the sun's orbit and the horizon, which varies as time passes. It is greatest, and therefore the time taken is least, when A is the position of the sun at the spring equinox.

Whether or not the Babylonians thought pictorially like this, they had a table for the time that each sign takes to rise. By adding them together six at a time they found the lengths of daylight when the sun was in each of the signs. It varied from 2/5 to 3/5 of a day, being inevitably half a day at the equinoxes.

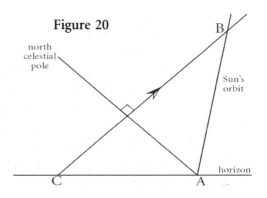

Figure 20

north celestial pole

Sun's orbit

horizon

C

A

B

Because the length of the longest day depends strictly on the latitude, if we know the latitude we can calculate the length of the longest day, and if we know the length of the longest day we can calculate the latitude. The Greeks found the length of the longest day at various places and recorded it in their geographical gazetteers, where we would have recorded the latitude. (Another thing that depends on the latitude is the elevation of the pole; in fact, they are equal. The Chinese, not knowing that the earth is round, had no concept of latitude. They recorded the elevation of the pole.)

PRECESSION

POLARIS HAS NOT ALWAYS been at the celestial north pole. The pole, in fact, traces a circle in the sky, but very slowly: it takes 26,000 years to complete the circle. This movement is called *precession*.

Because the movement is so slow it is hard to detect. The Babylonians and the very early Greeks did not know about it. It was discovered by Hipparchus about 130 BC. The Chinese discovered it just after AD 300.

To visualize this movement, imagine a model of the solar system on a tabletop with the sun in the middle and the earth moving round it in its orbit. The axis around which the earth spins is not vertical; its angle to the vertical is the obliquity. The direction of the axis in space does not remain fixed as time passes. While remaining at practically the same angle to the vertical it rotates very slowly around the vertical direction. It is rather like the motion of a spinning top. Modern dynamical theory explains both motions, calling them both *precession*.

Imagine a vertical line through the model sun. As the model earth moves around it the axis of spin will, at the instant of solstice, intersect this line. In the course of a year the direction of the axis will have changed by 1/26,000 of a revolution, so the position of the solstice will have changed by this amount. It takes the earth about twenty minutes to cover the distance from the new solstice to the old one. So it takes twenty minutes more for the earth to get back to the same position in space than to go from solstice to solstice. The time taken to get back to the same position in space is called a *sidereal year*. The ordinary solstice-to-solstice year is called a *tropical* year when it is important to distinguish the two. From the earth's point of view, the sidereal year is the time taken for the sun to get back to the same position against the starry background. (The word 'tropical' here has nothing to do with being warm. It comes from the Greek *tropos*, a turning-point – the solstice is the moment when the sun's north-to-south movement turns around.)

Although the visualization I have just described had the stars fixed and the poles moving, the Greeks thought of precession the other way round. To them, the poles were fixed and the stars were moving: the heavens were rotating slowly around an axis perpendicular to the sun's orbit, so that each star is moving round a circle parallel to the plane of the sun's orbit.

Hipparchus did not discover precession by measuring the motion of the celestial pole directly. As the pole moves against the starry background, so do the points where the plane of the equator crosses the sun's orbit, i.e. the points where the sun is at the equinoxes. Hipparchus found that the star Spica was 8° west of the spring equinox point, though 150 years earlier it had been 6° west. He investigated other stars and concluded cautiously that stars move westward at a rate not less than one degree in 100 years. Unfortunately, Ptolemy took the rate to be exactly one degree in 100 years (the correct value is one degree in 72 years) and confirmed this value by miscalculations of his own.

Because of Ptolemy's poor results, later western astronomers thought that the rate of precession varied appreciably over time. It was not until just before AD 1600 that its value was found accurately (by Brahe). In fact, it does vary very slightly in an 18.6-year cycle, and it is largely this that accounts for the slight change in the length of the year.

We do not know how the Chinese discovered precession. The *Shoushi* almanac of AD 1200 gave lengths for the sidereal and tropical years which imply a rate of one degree in 68 years.

Indian astronomers mostly ignored precession, but just after AD 600 Bhaskara quoted figures which imply a rate of one degree in 63 years.

SUNSPOTS

THE CHINESE SAW SUNSPOTS as early as 29 BC by looking through thin slices of jade. No western observers saw sunspots until the fourteenth century, when two sightings were reported from Russia. Sunspots have only recently been explained, the explanation being in the realm of astrophysics rather than astronomy.

THE VIEW FROM THE TROPICS

SO FAR, I have been describing what people in Europe, the middle East, China, or India see. But people living near the equator, such as the Mayas, the Incas or the Aztecs, see somewhat different phenomena. The annual progress of sunset or sunrise along the horizon is pretty much what I have been describing except that the angle between extreme sunrises or extreme sunsets would be fairly small. But this cycle does not tie in with the midday height of the sun, though it does tie in roughly with the weather – the rainy season comes at about the same time each year.

At midday in midsummer the sun will be north, not south, of a Mayan or Aztec observer, even though both are in the northern hemisphere. As the days pass, the elevation of the sun at midday increases until one day the sun is vertically overhead at midday. Astronomers call this the day of *zenith passage*. From then on the sun at midday is south of the observer and its elevation decreases until at midwinter the midday sun is at its lowest. The process then reverses.

Very probably early anthropologists working with the Incas confused the zenith passage with the equinox and thought that the Incas were talking about the equinox, which would in fact have held no interest for them, when they were actually talking about the zenith passage.

Archaeologists have found vertical shafts in some Mayan ruins which they think might have been used for observing the zenith passage, though watching the shadow of a vertical rod shrink to zero would be much easier.

ECLIPSES

A TOTAL ECLIPSE of the sun is spectacular. But total eclipses are rare. How many have you seen? (If you were warned in advance and deliberately went to a place where the eclipse was total, that doesn't count.) To deal in any detail with eclipses, we will have to wait until we have studied the moon.

It is fairly natural for primitive people to find a total eclipse of the sun a frightening experience. Some were also frightened by eclipses of the moon: and not only primitive tribes, but such civilized nations as the Incas. According to Garcilaso de la Vega, who wrote extensively about the Incas, they thought that when the moon was eclipsed it was ill. They were seized with fear when an eclipse began, and sounded all the instruments that they could lay their hands on to make a noise, even beating their dogs to make them yelp, in the belief that this would awaken the moon from the sleep caused by her sickness.

2

The Sky and the Stars

HE SKY AT NIGHT looks like the inside of a dome. The stars all seem to be at the same distance from us and it takes imagination to wonder whether they might not be. The only early astronomer who showed this much initiative is Geminus, around AD 70, who said that we must not take it for granted that the stars lie on a sphere, and it is because our sight can reach only so far that the differences between the distances of the stars are imperceptible. But he was the odd man out. Eudoxus, Ptolemy and Aryabhata had the stars quite definitely on a sphere whose centre is the earth. Ptolemy indeed was so confident about this that he gave it as a reason for believing that the earth is fixed at the centre of the universe – if it moved from the centre the night sky would not appear to be a hemisphere. A starry sphere is compatible with what other astronomers wrote, with two possible exceptions: Anaximander and the Chinese *gai tian* theory.

Anaximander may have thought that the stars lie on a cylinder rather than a sphere – more details later on page 87.

The Chinese theory in the *Zhou bi* described on page 11 has a flat earth and sky, but another section of the *Zhou bi* has the sky like a rain-hat over an earth shaped like an upturned pan. A reference to this theory has the sky like a canopy over a chariot. This theory has been called *gai tian* (*gai* = canopy, *tian* = sky).

Luckily, distances are not important for the main early uses of astronomy, namely for navigation, astrology, and devising a calendar. The mariner's sextant measures only angles, not distances. And when astrologers say that Mars is 'in Aries', Mars is only in the same direction from the earth as the sign Aries.

THE CELESTIAL SPHERE

HOW CAN WE PINPOINT the position of an object in the sky? If distances don't matter, we have only to define its direction. But directions are hard to define. Modern mathematicians use vectors, but the ancients did not have vectors – not even the Greeks, who were top-notch geometers.

The solution is that if the distance doesn't matter we might as well take all the objects to be at the same distance from the earth, in which case they will all lie on a sphere whose centre is the earth. A sphere used in this way is called the *celestial sphere*: the celestial sphere is a large imaginary sphere whose centre is the centre of the earth. Whether or not this sphere is the one on which the stars seem to lie does not matter in the slightest.

Every point on the sphere has a direction from the earth; every direction from the earth leads to a point on the sphere. So we can use points on the sphere to denote directions.

The Greeks (and, following them, the Indians and the Arabs) developed a spherical geometry and trigonometry which let them make sophisticated calculations. Even when they discovered that things were not all the same distance from the earth – and that the distance from the earth of the sun, the moon, and each planet varied – they still used the sphere. So for them the ecliptic was not the actual orbit of the sun but its projection on the celestial sphere. The name *ecliptic* comes from the fact that it is only when the moon is very near to this plane that an eclipse can occur, because only then are the sun, moon and earth in line. It is this circle, rather than the sun's orbit itself, that the Greeks divided into twelve signs. The first sign, the Ram, started at the point where the sun appeared to be at the spring equinox.

The north and south celestial poles are now the points where the axis around which the sky turns relative to the earth intersects the celestial sphere, and the celestial equator is the circle in which the plane of the equator cuts the celestial sphere. Consequently the points where the sun appears to be at the equinoxes are the points where the ecliptic and the celestial equator cross.

The Greeks set up systems of coordinates on the celestial sphere. The angular distance of a point on the ecliptic from the spring equinox point is its (celestial) *longitude*. The *longitude* of any point on the celestial sphere is the longitude of the point on the ecliptic nearest to it. (The poles do not have a longitude.) The *latitude* of a point is its angular distance from the plane of the ecliptic.

Hipparchus used eclipses to find the longitudes of stars near the ecliptic. At the mid-point of an eclipse he measured the difference in longitude between the star and the moon. He calculated the longitude of the sun at the time from his theory of the motion of the sun. At the midpoint of an eclipse the longitude of the moon differs from this by exactly 180°. This gives the longitude of the moon, and then the measured difference gives the longitude of the star. (Why could he not use this method at any time, without waiting for an eclipse, by calculating directly the longitude of the moon? Because his theory of the motion of the moon was not accurate enough.)

In contrast to geography, celestial latitude is not measured from the equator but from the ecliptic. Astronomers do have a word for angular distance from the celestial equator: *declination*. Declinations south of the equator are negative. If we know the npd of a star, we can find its declination: just subtract the npd from a right angle. And vice versa. Angular distance round the equator is given the rather odd name *right ascension*.

The Chinese divided the sky into 28 regions called *xiu*, each named after a constellation. In each of these constellations they singled out a star as the leading star of the *xiu*. They watched the sky rotate. As it rotates each star passes due south of the observer once a day. A star due south of the observer was said to be 'centred'. A *xiu* consists of its leading star and those stars that are centred after the leading star but before the leading star of the next *xiu*. Stars that are centred in daylight at one date will be centred at night half a year later, so the whole visible sky can be divided up in this way. The time-intervals between the leading stars give the widths of the *xius*, which vary widely.

In the *gai tian* theory the edge of a *xiu* is a rib of the umbrella-shaped sky. (One writer mentioned that the canopy has 28 ribs.) The *xius* occupied by the sun at the solstices (which are assumed to divide the year exactly in half) and at the instants halfway between them are listed, giving us four points of the orbit of the sun on the canopy.

Later, the Chinese believed that the stars lie on a sphere. Then the edge of a *xiu* would be a semicircle stretching from one celestial pole to the other.

The Chinese described the position of a star by giving its npd, naming the *xiu* it lies in, and saying how far it is from the edge of the *xiu*.

The Indians divided the path of the moon into 27 or 28 segments called *nakshatras*. Unlike the *xius*, the *nakshatras* were all the same size. Later the Indians introduced the signs of the zodiac, which like the Babylonian ones and unlike the Greek ones, were fixed relative to the stars, not to the equinox points.

THE EFFECT OF PRECESSION

BECAUSE THE DISTANCE of a star from the ecliptic does not change, its latitude does not change as time passes, but its longitude does: it increases by one degree every 72 years. Precession affects npd and right ascension in a more complicated way, which can be calculated from the change in longitude by trigonometrical methods.

THE ASTROLABON

THE MOST USEFUL COORDINATES for following the motions of the sun, moon and planets are celestial latitude and longitude. How shall we measure them? We want to measure angular distances around and away from the ecliptic.

We can use the instrument shown in figure 10 (page 18) if we can find a way to set the basic circle in the plane of the ecliptic. We do this as follows.

We take the version of the instrument in which the axis round which it rotates points to the pole, and fix to the rotating ring another ring of the same size at an angle to the plane of the equator equal to the obliquity of the ecliptic. This means that as it rotates around the axis it can be swung into the plane of the ecliptic. I call it the ecliptic ring.

To swing it into the plane of the ecliptic we use the fact that the sun is on the ecliptic. We wait for a sunny day (the Greeks may not have had to wait very long) and turn the instrument until the ecliptic ring overshadows itself.

We fit the instrument with a rotating ring, perpendicular to the ecliptic ring, and fitted with sights. We can now measure latitudes and longitudes.

You can probably see the snag. We can only set the instrument up in this way in daylight, but the stars come out at night. The Chinese overcame this snag by equipping the instrument with a clockwork mechanism which made it turn at the rate of one revolution per day. (They had clockwork from about AD 700.) The Greeks had no clockwork; instead they used their ingenuity.

They equipped their instrument with an extra ring, rotating in the same way as the sighting ring (but not fitted with sights). If we know the longitude of the moon we can set the extra ring to the known longitude of the moon (on the ecliptic ring) and turn the instrument until the extra ring is aligned on the moon. The instrument is now set, and we can measure the latitude and longitude of a star. We cannot measure a whole lot of stars because that would take time and the longitude of the moon is changing all the while. However, once we have measured the longitude of one star we can set the extra ring to its longitude, and align it on the star. Then we can measure as many stars as we like at our leisure.

There remains the problem of finding the longitude of the moon. The

Greek theory of the motion of the moon was not accurate enough to give good results by setting the extra ring to the calculated longitude and aligning it. So they waited until a day when the moon was visible just before sunset and found its longitude then, using the sun to set the instrument. Then they waited until the stars came out. The Greeks were able to calculate the change in longitude in this short interval accurately enough. This gave the longitude of the moon after dark.

Ptolemy described an instrument of this type in the *Syntaxis*. It differed a little from the description above. Instead of a sighting-rod, the sighting-ring was equipped with two sights at diametrically-opposite points on a ring that slid round inside it. The extra ring, pivoted in the same way as the sighting-ring, was outside the rotating framework. The whole set-up was quite complicated. It was called an *astrolabon*.

It was rather an awkward instrument. The extra ring outside the framework could not turn freely; the pivots got in the way. And the ring sliding inside the sighting-ring must have been only too likely to jam.

LATER INSTRUMENTS

BOTH EASTERN AND WESTERN astronomers came to realize that instruments with complicated pivots were inefficient: if the pivots were not inconveniently tight the instrument would wobble enough to destroy its accuracy. Tycho Brahe had, just before AD 1600, the giant armilla, nearly 3 metres in diameter, shown in figure 11 (page 19). It consisted of a single ring pivoting around the pole-to-pole axis, fitted with a sighting-rod that measured npds. The position of the ring, measured on the fixed semicircular scale round its middle, gave distances round the celestial equator, from which right ascensions could be found.

The Chinese had, just before AD 1300, an instrument whose name literally means 'simplified instrument'. The main part is a ring (smaller than Tycho's) pivoting round the pole-to-pole axis and fitted with a sighting-tube. The scale for measuring positions round the equator is at the bottom and is a complete circle. It can turn about its centre, being fitted with roller bearings, and is marked with the *xius*.

THE CLEVER GREEKS

THE GREEKS took the opposite tack. Instead of large simplified instruments they devised small complicated ones. For example, a metal box was found in a ship that probably sank some time between 100 BC and 1 BC. It contained thirty or more gear-wheels, and was designed to show positions on the ecliptic. It is too badly damaged to be reconstructed completely. Another instrument, probably dating from just after AD 500 is better preserved; one wheel has 59 teeth. It was designed to show the phases of the moon and the longitudes of the moon and of the sun.

But the best known of the ingenious Greek instruments is the astrolabe.

Theon of Smyrna mentioned the astrolabe around AD 500, though no specimens as old as this survive. The National Maritime Museum in England has over fifty specimens dating from AD 1230 to about AD 1700.

The astrolabe is a map of the celestial sphere. Making a flat map of the celestial sphere is like making a flat map of the spherical earth in an atlas. Atlases use many different ways of mapping the earth – many different *projections*. The one most commonly used for the astrolabe is the south polar projection.

To see how this projection works, imagine a small model of the celestial sphere. A point P on this sphere is joined to the south celestial pole S, and the point P* where the line joining them crosses the plane of the equator is the projection of P, as shown in figure 21. Clearly circles on the celestial sphere parallel to the equator project into circles; those south of the equator into circles larger than the equator, those north of the equator into circles smaller than the equator. These include the *tropics*: the two through the most northerly and southerly points of the ecliptic. The map is usually large enough to contain the tropic of Capricorn (the southern tropic). The centre of these circles is the projection of the north celestial pole.

Vertical and horizontal coordinates are also mapped. Let Z be the observer's zenith on the sphere. Imagine the sphere furnished with vertical circles through Z and with horizontal circles. (They would look like the meridians of longitude and parallels of latitude on a globe, with Z playing the part of the north pole and the horizon playing the part of the equator.) The parts of these lines above the horizon are mapped. The map looks something like an unusually regular spider's web, as shown in figure 22. Its position depends on the latitude of the observer, and some astrolabes have several maps for use

south polar projection

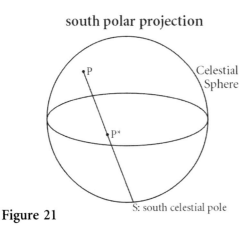

Figure 21

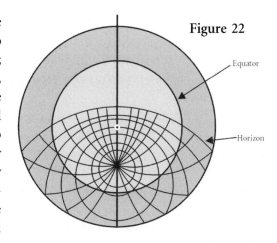

Figure 22

Equator

Horizon

A plate for an astrolabe for latitude 30° north

at more than one site. These projections are engraved onto brass plates (by calculation; not by using a model sphere, of course). The projections are all circles; the fact that all circles on the sphere map into circles was never formally stated but it follows easily from a clever piece of geometry by Apollonius. The projection of a horizontal circle is usually called by its arabic name *almucantar*. Each is marked with the appropriate elevation.

The astrolabe consists of a circular brass plate with a raised rim into which the maps are fitted. It is provided with a suspension-ring and a sighting rod pivoted at the centre, like the portable instrument described on page 18.

The line joining the projection of the north pole (the centre of the map) to the projection of the zenith is set vertically in the astrolabe. The map is symmetrical about this line. Sometimes the rim of the astrolabe is graduated in degrees, with this line marking the zero.

A map of the ecliptic and of some twenty to fifty bright stars is fitted inside the rim and over the map described above, and is able to rotate about its centre, to follow the rotation of the sky. It is usually called by its Latin name *rete*, which means 'web'.

If we were making one today we would probably make it of glass or transparent plastic, but medieval ones were made of brass. A *rete* consists of a brass ring which fits inside the rim of the astrolabe with a thin brass circle representing the ecliptic and thin brass curved strips carrying

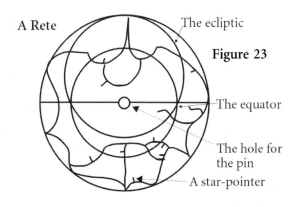

A Rete

The ecliptic

Figure 23

The equator

The hole for the pin

A star-pointer

pointers that mark the positions of stars, whose names are engraved on the strips. Figure 23 shows the general idea. You can see why it is called a 'web'. It usually has a strip across the middle holding a small ring which fits round a pin in the middle of the astrolabe; both the *rete* and the sighting-rod turn around this pin.

To set the astrolabe for a given time and date, measure the elevation of the sun. Find the longitude of the sun at the date in question; some astrolabes are engraved with conversion scales on the back from which this can be read off. Turn the *rete* until the point P on the ecliptic with this longitude is against the *almucantar* corresponding to the sun's elevation. The astrolabe is now set.

The angle between the line from the centre to P and the line marking south gives the time before or after noon; it can be read off from the degree scale round the rim at the rate of 15° = 1 hour. To make this easier, the sighting-rod is usually designed so that one edge passes exactly through the centre of the astrolabe. A typical shape is shown in figure 24. Turn the rod until this edge passes through P and read off where it crosses the scale.

Figure 24: A sighting-rod for an astrolabe. Each vane, a small rectangle perpendicular to the plane of the paper, is pierced with a small hole in the centre.

To find the time of sunrise, turn the *rete* until P is on the eastern part of the horizon *almucantar* and read off the time as above. For sunset, use the western part of the *almucantar*.

At night the astrolabe can be set by using the elevation of a star.

Other things that can be found using an astrolabe include the times at which a star rises or sets, the positions of the horizon at which it does so, and its elevation when it is due south. The astrolabe can also be used to find the positions of stars at a given time and date (for casting horoscopes).

In the sixteenth century astrolabes were devised which can be used at different latitudes. They were called universal astrolabes and were based on the *lamina universal* devised by Ali bin Khalaf of Toledo, shortly after AD 1000. They are described in the National Maritime Museum's booklet *The planispheric astrolabe.*

THE STARS

TO EARLY PEOPLE the stars were points of light, forming patterns in the sky, which rotate around the pole-to-pole axis, while the patterns remain unchanged. There are five exceptions – the planets. This word comes from the Greek for 'wanderer'. The other stars, by contrast, are called 'fixed stars'. (Nowadays we do not count the planets as stars, but we do consider the sun to be one.)

Most early people took it for granted that the patterns formed by the stars are fixed, but Ptolemy carefully compared positions in his time with positions described by Hipparchus some three hundred years earlier. Because trios of stars that were in line in Hipparchus's time were still in line, Ptolemy concluded that the patterns did not change. In fact, the 'fixed' stars do move relative to each other, but the movement is so tiny that it was not detected until just after AD 1700. It is called 'proper motion'.

Ptolemy seems to have had a particular reason for this comparison. Every one of the alignments that he cited involved at least one star near the ecliptic and at least one star well off the ecliptic. He obviously wanted to check that the whole celestial sphere underwent precession. Hipparchus, using the method described on page 35, had confirmed precession only for stars near the ecliptic, but if only stars near the ecliptic underwent precession the alignments that Ptolemy cited from Hipparchus would be destroyed.

CONSTELLATIONS

ALL OVER THE WORLD people grouped the stars into constellations, to which they gave fanciful names. The north-west Amerindians saw a sculpin (a local fish) in the sky, south African tribes saw gemsbok, and so on.

Different people grouped the stars in different ways. For example, the Babylonian constellation *Iku* (field) consisted of four stars arranged more or less in a square. The Greeks incorporated one of these stars in their constellation Andromeda and the other three in Pegasus. But at least two patterns are striking enough for a number of different people to group them together. One of these is formed by the seven brightest stars in the Greek constellation Orion, shown in figure 25. Very many people group the three central stars (Orion's belt) as a constellation, and quite a number recognize all seven as a constellation, including the Egyptians, who called it *Sahu* and identified it with the god Osiris. The three central stars were his genitals.

Another striking pattern is the one shown in figure 26. It looks like a long-handled pan and the Chinese name for it means 'northern ladle'. In the west it is known as the Big Dipper, Charles's Wain, or the Plough. A number of North American tribes saw it, or rather the four stars in a rough square, as a bear, and the three other stars as hunters. The Micmacs, for example, called it *Mouhinne*, which means 'bear', and a similar but smaller constellation *Mouhinchiche*, the diminutive of *Mouhinne*. Very surprisingly the Greeks also saw these constellations as bears. Modern astronomers use the Latin translations of the Greek names: Ursa major [greater she-bear] and Ursa minor.

Figure 25: The seven brightest stars in Orion

The most likely (or perhaps least unlikely) explanation is that the constellations were originally recognized by a Siberian tribe who crossed the Bering strait when north America was populated, and the Greeks picked it up from some tribe like the Scythians. For some reason, the Greeks saw the three 'hunters' as a tail, so pictures based on the Greek description, such as the one in figure 27, look more like a giant raccoon than a bear.

Grouping the stars into constellations has nothing to do with astronomy as a science. Or has it? Perhaps some of the constellations were part of a primitive system of coordinates in the sky. The Greek constellation Hydra, for example, consists of a long wavy line of rather dim stars that no-one would naturally form into a picture, but it lay along the celestial equator around 2000 BC. (Because of precession it no longer does.)

The suggestion that the Greek constellations were originally devised much earlier than the classical Greek period is bolstered by the shape of the space round the south celestial pole where the Greeks had no named constellations. If the Greeks had

Figure 26: The Big Dipper

Figure 27
Ursa Major

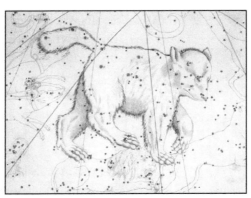

devised constellations from their own observations, say around 500 BC, the blank space would have been symmetrical about the pole of that date; it would have been the region inside a circle whose centre is the pole and whose south polar distance is the latitude of Greece. But it is not. On one side, the Greek constellations Ara, Centaurus and Argo come within 20° of the pole at that date; on the other side, the nearest constellations are 60° away. In fact, the blank space is roughly oval and covers both the region invisible to the ancient Greeks and the region invisible from the same latitude in 2000 BC.

About 350 BC Aratus wrote a poetical description of the constellations, based on a work by Eudoxus. Hipparchus criticized many details in this description. But many of the things he criticized, though wrong in his time, were right around 2000 BC, the difference being due to precession. Evidently Eudoxus had described earlier observations instead of making his own. In particular, he said that Hydra lies along the celestial equator. And he did not mention Canopus, the second brightest star (Sirius is the brightest) which was not visible from Greece in 2000 BC but was in classical times. It is ironic that the man who made this criticism was the man who discovered precession, the cause of the discrepancy.

The data are not precise enough for us to say where the early observations were made. They could have been made anywhere at about the right latitude, perhaps Crete or Phoenicia.

CATALOGUES

BETWEEN 370 AND 270 BC the Chinese compiled three catalogues of stars, giving their positions in the sky in the way described on page 39. Between them these catalogues listed nearly 1,500 stars. They have not survived, but were used about AD 300 to make a map of the sky.

Ptolemy's *Syntaxis* contained a catalogue of just over a thousand stars. Although Ptolemy claimed to have observed them himself, internal evidence shows that he brought up to date a catalogue made some three hundred years earlier by altering the longitudes to allow for precession. The evidence also shows that the latitudes and longitudes of the southern stars were calculated from measurements of the npd and one other coordinate (most probably the right ascension).

Arabic astronomers made a number of maps and catalogues of stars, using the Greek constellations. The earlier ones were made by bringing the one in the *Syntaxis* up to date, but shortly after AD 1400, Ulugh Beg made his own catalogue.

Just after AD 1600, Tycho Brahe compiled a catalogue which was about ten times as accurate as previous ones, though it did not quite contain the thousand stars that he claimed, once mistakes and duplicates are removed. There are several reasons for Brahe's remarkable accuracy. His greatly improved instruments helped. He did not measure latitude and longitude but declination and right ascension, which he converted to latitude and longitude mathematically. He therefore did not need the ingenious but complicated astrolabon; he used a simpler but larger instrument like the one in figure 11 (page 19). Brahe found his coordinates with this instrument in the way that the Greeks found latitude and longitude, but using Venus instead of the moon. There are two advantages to this: Venus, being just a point of light as seen from the earth, can be located more precisely than the moon, and its motion is more regular than the moon's.

HELIACAL RISINGS

AS FIGURE 15 (page 25) shows, the sky seen at the same time over a number of nights rotates slowly. It takes a sidereal year to complete a revolution. From the viewpoint of the earth this means that the sun takes a sidereal year to travel once round the ecliptic and back to its starting-point against the starry background. The sky takes about four minutes to turn from its position at midnight to its position at the previous midnight.

Suppose that we are watching a star rise just before dawn. The next day, the star will rise some four minutes earlier but dawn will be almost the same time – one day does not make much difference to the length of daylight. After half a year the star will be rising around sunset and after a year it will be back again to rising just before dawn. So by watching the stars we can tell when a year has passed. (When we get down to precise details we find that the time from one rising at dawn to the next is neither a tropical year nor a sidereal year, but is pretty close to both.)

If a star rises exactly at sunrise it will be swamped by the light of the sun. The first rising that can be seen is called the *heliacal* rising. The heliacal risings of stars can be used as a calendar. For example, Hesiod's *Works and Days*, written about 800 BC, recommends picking grapes at the heliacal rising of Arcturus: 'when rose-fingered dawn looks on Arcturus'. We do not know whether Greek farmers actually did this instead of picking their grapes when they were good and ripe. In England before the introduction of modern scientific farming, a farmer might tell when to plant by digging a hole in the ground in early spring and putting his elbow in it. If it was too cold, he waited; if not, he planted.

However, the Hopi (in the southwestern USA) found it useful to use astronomy to date planting. They knew that crops planted more than a few days after the summer solstice would not survive the frosts in the autumn. They had 'sun-watchers' who found the solstice by watching sunsets. And, as we saw on page 6, the Incas also timed planting by using astronomy.

The Egyptians noticed that the flooding of the Nile, so important for Egyptian agriculture, took place just after the heliacal rising of Sirius. When they devised a calendar they started the year at that date. They listed 36 groups of stars, which we call *decans*, each decan having its heliacal rising some ten days after the previous one. On any one night, each decan rises about 40 minutes after the previous one, so by watching the decans rise the Egyptians could tell the time at night.

The decans were arranged in tables. The first column showed twelve decans that rose on one particular night. The second column showed the decans that rose ten days later. The first decan in the first column was then rising before sunset and could not be seen; the second decan was then rising at sunset and took its place at the head of the column, and every decan moved up one place, a new decan appearing at the bottom. Each decan appears in a diagonal line across the table, giving the tables their usual name: diagonal calendars. They are found – believe it or not – inside the lids of coffins.

In fact, heliacal rising is mentioned surprisingly early, considering that it is rather a subtle concept. Hesiod is not the first: in the *Iliad*, probably first written down some time before 700 BC, Homer described Sirius as a 'star of waning summer' showing that he knew at least that different stars are visible at different times of the year. Hesiod goes into great detail. He mentions that Arcturus rises sixty days after the winter solstice (and is followed by the return of the swallows). After Sirius has risen it was believed to influence people: women are full of lust and men are feeble. (I wonder if he really believed that.) When Orion and Sirius are high in the sky at dawn and Arcturus rises it is the time to pick grapes (as noted above). The setting of the Pleiades and Orion heralds the stormy season. Hesiod also mentions the equinox as the date when day and night are equal.

One early Greek writer, Autolycus, about 320 BC, went into the theory of rising very thoroughly. He showed that rising at sunrise and rising at sunset occur half a year apart, and so do the two corresponding settings. He investigated the order in which these risings and settings occurred; it depends on whether the star is north or south of the ecliptic. Because these risings and settings cannot be seen, all this is of theoretical importance only.

Heliacal rising, which can be seen, is the first time that rising is visible after the sunrise rising. Autolycus assumed that the interval between them was 15 days. In fact, the interval varies; it depends on many factors including the angle between the ecliptic and the horizon, and even on such intangibles as how keen the observer's eyesight is. Autolycus investigated the last visible rising just before the sunset rising, and the two similar settings. He showed that a star well north of the ecliptic (but not so far north that it never sets) will, during part of the year, rise before sunrise, be invisible during the day, and set in the evening. A star well south of the ecliptic (but not so far south that it never rises) will, during part of the year, be seen to rise, be seen to set, and to be visible all the time between rising and setting. A star near the ecliptic will, during part of the year, appear in the sky just after sunset (having risen in daylight) and be visible until just before sunrise.

PRECESSION AND THE PYRAMIDS

PRECESSION MAY HAVE AFFECTED the orientation of early Egyptian pyramids including the famous three at Giza.

These pyramids are oriented amazingly accurately. Their sides run almost exactly east-to-west and north-to-south. For example, the sides of the pyramid of Khufu (known as the 'great pyramid') are out of alignment by 2½, 2, 5½ and 2½ minutes of arc. A minute of arc is one-sixtieth of a degree, so they are all out by less than one-tenth of a degree.

However, if we arrange the pyramids in order, starting with the earliest, we find that with two exceptions (which I will return to later) the north-to-south orientations turn steadily eastwards, as shown by the table below, which shows the deviation from north (in minutes of arc) of the east side.

◻ Snofru's pyramid at Meidum   21′ west

◻	'Bent' pyramid at Dahshur	17′ west
◻	North pyramid at Dahshur	9′ west
◻	Khufu's pyramid at Giza	5½′ west
◻	Khafre's pyramid at Giza	exception
◻	Menkaure's pyramid at Giza	12′ east
◻	Sahure's pyramid at Abusir	exception
◻	Neferirkare's pyramid at Abusir	30′ east

Although we are not absolutely sure of the intervals of time between the pyramids, because we are not sure of the lengths of reigns of the pharaohs, these figures are consistent with the orientation changing at a constant rate.

Why would this be? Think of the way that we find north today. We look for the 'Big Dipper' (shown in figure 26 on page 46) and follow the 'pointers' to a bright star, Polaris, which is very close to the pole: in fact it is often called the Pole Star or the North Star.

We are lucky in having a star close to the pole. In ancient times there wasn't one. But even without a pole star we could still use the pointers as long as we know that the pole is on the line joining them. We simply wait until they are aligned vertically; they are then due north. The early Polynesians and Micronesians navigating between the islands in the south Pacific ocean used this principle: when the Southern Cross is vertical it is due south.

The Egyptians may have used this principle too. In their day – to be precise in 2,467 BC – the pole was on the line joining two reasonably bright stars: Kochab and Mizar. If the Egyptians had found the pole (perhaps by a method like the one explained on page 18) they could then have oriented the pyramids on these two. But there is a snag.

Because of precession the pole will move relative to the stars and will therefore move off the line joining Kochab to Mizar. This line will then not be due north when it is vertical. If Kochab is above Mizar the line will drift to the east, if Mizar is above Kochab it will drift to the west, at the same rate. It looks as though six of the pyramids were aligned with Kochab above Mizar. Not only that, but Khafre's pyramid is 6 minutes east of north and Sahure's 23 minutes east of north, so they are out by the right amount in the wrong direction. Therefore they could have been oriented with Mizar above Kochab. The dates at which the alignment gives the actual orientations of the pyramids can be calculated and give reasonable intervals between the dates of the pyramids.

This is not the only possibility. Any astronomical method of orienting the pyramids that is affected by precession will have the same effect. One suggestion that has been made is that having found north the Egyptians could find south, east and west, and could look for a star that rises due east. Precession would make it rise gradually further south and account for the drift in orientation. The two exceptions would have to be aligned on the position at which the star sets. But this would not work for Khafre's pyramid. The plateau at Giza slopes up to the west and when the Egyptians levelled the ground for Khafre's pyramid they left a stone wall to the west. This blocks the view of the far horizon, and as a star disappears from view behind the wall it is much too far south to account for the slight deviation of Khafre's pyramid.

NAVIGATING BY THE STARS

THE POSITION at which a star sets does not change like the position of sunset. There is no day-to-day change in a yearly cycle; the star sets at the same place each day, though this place does move (very slowly) as the years pass because of precession. The same applies to risings. This change means that an archaeologist who is investigating the alignment of a structure to the rising or setting of a star has to know approximately the date of the structure.

It is not easy to see a star set. As it sinks it grows dimmer and only the brightest stars can be seen right down to a flat horizon. However, Polynesians and Micronesians, who made long voyages in the Pacific ocean, used the stars to help navigate. A star high overhead is not useful for showing a direction in which to travel, but a star near the horizon is. The sailors chose a star that rose or set in the same direction as the island they were aiming for, and pointed their canoe towards it. When it rose too high to be useful or sank too low to be seen, they switched to another star that rose or set at the same point of the horizon. If another star was not soon available they made allowance for the sideways movement of the guiding star as it rose or set obliquely, a movement much less than it would be for voyagers further from the equator; in fact a voyager right on the equator sees stars rise and set vertically, with no sideways movement at all. It was rare to need more than ten stars in one night. To use this method to get from, say, Samoa to the Cook islands, they would need a succession of stars that rose in the same direction as the Cook islands from Samoa. However, they could also use stars to one side of the destination; one sailing instruction called for keeping the Southern Cross on the port bow.

The navigators knew that the Pole Star is due north and that although the Southern Cross is some distance from the celestial south pole, when it becomes upright as it circles the pole it is pretty well due south.

A modern compass-card has round its edge 'north', 'north-north-east' etc. Round the edge of a Polynesian or Micronesian equivalent you would see the native names of the stars that rose or set in the various directions. (Presumably these star-compasses were made after the introduction of writing to the Pacific islands.)

A canoe does not go in the direction in which it is pointing unless the wind is squarely behind it and there is no cross-current, but from the angle between the wake and the direction to the guiding star it is possible to judge the amount of leeway. And some sailing instructions made allowance for local winds and currents.

The navigators also noted which stars passed vertically overhead. This would tell them how far north or south they were. (If they were on the equator, only stars on the celestial equator could pass vertically overhead. If they were 10° north of the equator, only stars 10° north of the equator could pass overhead, and so on; the further north a star rose or set, the further north they would have to be for it to pass vertically overhead.)

Besides astronomy the navigators used all the local knowledge that they had picked up over the years, including such things as the habits of sea-birds. And some less reliable lore: a navigator would pluck an eye-lash; if it came out easily, land was near.

3

The Moon

W HAT STRIKES US MOST when we look at the moon? Its change of shape, from crescent to half-moon to full moon and back. Why does the moon change shape?

The first thing that people had to understand was that when we see a crescent moon, the crescent is not all there is; the rest of the moon is still there but because it is dark we cannot see it; we see only the part lit by the sun. Aristotle was quite clear about this: he reported that he had seen the moon approach Mars, which disappeared behind the dark edge and reappeared on the bright side. Very occasionally, when the conditions are just right, we can dimly see the rest of the disc: 'the old moon in the new moon's arms'.

It might have taken early people quite an effort to realise that the moon was lit by the sun because it goes against the obvious fact that in daytime the sun is above the horizon and there is sunshine, whereas at night the sun is below the horizon and there is no sunshine. However, we can often see the moon in daylight and it doesn't suddenly change at sunset. And the shapes of the moon as it goes through its phases are the same as the shapes that you see if you shine a light on a white ball from various angles.

There is one snag. Imagine that it is just before sunset, with the sun just above the horizon and the moon about half-full and high in the sky. It is easy to judge whether the almost straight edge of the half-moon is tilted to the left or to the right. If you try this, you will see from the tilt that light is falling on the moon from slightly above the horizontal. But the moon is high in the sky and the sun is low, so how can the light falling on the moon be coming from the sun? Well, the sun is so much further away than the moon that the line from the moon to the sun is practically parallel to the line from you to the sun; the sun is actually higher than the moon, though it looks lower.

One early thinker who did not understand any of this was Anaximander. His moon was, like his sun, a hole in a tube encircling the earth. Presumably the tube was filled with something that gave out a silvery glow. The opening and closing of the hole made the shape of the visible moon vary.

The earliest Greek statement that the moon shines by reflected sunlight is by Parmenides (512 to 540 BC). The Chinese realized at some time between 300 and 100 BC that 'the sun gives the moon its appearance'.

ECLIPSES

'I was out last night. Beautiful full moon. But something weird happened. It disappeared.'

'Completely?'

'No, a faint red glow was left. After a while the moon reappeared.'

Some such conversation must have taken place many times in early days. Of course, our star-gazer was describing an eclipse of the moon. After a while people would discover more details. This happens only at full moon; never when the moon is clearly less than full. It starts with something taking a circular bite out of the moon on the left-hand side (the right-hand side for Australians and other people living in the southern hemisphere), which gradually becomes larger, moving across the moon to the right until the whole moon is devoured. The eclipse ends with an ever-decreasing bite on the right.

Sometimes the bite moves across the top or bottom of the moon and does not cover the whole moon. These eclipses are *partial* and are fairly easy to see if you look for them. Even partial eclipses never take place on two full moons in succession (well, hardly ever).

The usual interval between two successive eclipses is six months, with five months noticeably rarer. Sometimes it is eleven or twelve months, or even longer.

Almanacs give the dates of eclipses. But they can give a misleading impression. People would not see eclipses nearly as regularly as the entries in an almanac, in which two successive eclipses are rarely more than six months apart.

For example, a nearly total eclipse was visible from the west coast of north America in March 1997. Six months later there was another eclipse but it was not visible from America (it was visible from China). Five months later there was what almanacs describe as a *penumbral* eclipse. It was well described by the *Griffith Observer*, which says that the moon did not darken enough to notice and that the event, though listed in almanacs, was virtually unobservable. There was another penumbral eclipse a month later.

Five months after that, something more subtle happened: an eclipse with such a small bite taken out of the moon that (again according to the *Griffith Observer*) 'in practice, no eclipse can be seen'.

Six months after that there was a more clearly visible partial eclipse. So unless someone saw the very tiny eclipse, the interval between the eclipses that a sky-watcher saw was 23 months.

The Babylonians used eclipses for astrological forecasts. For example, 'If an eclipse begins on the 14th of Duzu in the south, a great king will die; if it begins in the east, rains and floods will be regular.' (Duzu is the fourth month of the Babylonian year.)

WHAT CAUSES ECLIPSES?

ANAXIMANDER THOUGHT that the closing-up of the hole in the sun-tube that lets out sunlight causes eclipses of the sun. Whether he thought that the closing of the hole in the moon-tube causes eclipses of the moon as well as the monthly change of shape is not clear. The earliest mention of the true cause of eclipses is by Anaxagoras, who was born just before 500 BC: eclipses of the moon are caused by the earth's shadow falling on the moon, which can happen only at full moon; eclipses of the sun are caused by the moon coming between the earth and the sun, and can happen only at new moon.

The Babylonians, too, knew that eclipses of the sun took place only at new moon and eclipses of the moon only at full moon.

In fact, once people realised that the phases of the moon are caused by the sun shining on it at different angles and that eclipses of the moon take place only at full moon, this explanation is fairly obvious.

It is now possible to explain penumbral eclipses. Because the sun is not a point, it is possible for a point on the moon to be hidden by the earth from only part of the sun. It will be in partial shadow, the *penumbra*, like the stretch from C to D in figure 4 on page 15. Figure 28 (not to scale) shows the situation.

The Chinese knew by 20 BC how eclipses were caused, but astronomers had a hard job convincing philosophers who, as late as AD 100, maintained that because the moon is *yin* and therefore weak it could not possibly eclipse the sun, which is *yang* and therefore strong.

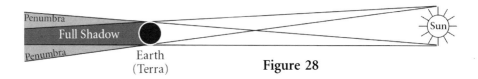

Figure 28

Early Indian astronomers believed that at an eclipse the sun is swallowed by one of two celestial dragons, *rahu* and *ketu*, which lurk at the points where the moon's orbit on the celestial sphere crosses the sun's.

When you come to think of it, those two dragons would have to behave in a very odd way. When the sun and the moon are both close to one dragon it devours the sun. When the sun is close to one dragon and the moon is close to the other, the one close to the moon devours it.

MONTHS

THE BABYLONIANS were the first people to make accurate measurements of the motion of the moon. This had two practical purposes. One was to find the times at which the moon rises and sets. The other was to forecast the date of each new moon – they made each calendar month start on the day of the new moon and it is obviously a nuisance to have to wait until the moon actually appears before you know what the date is.

The Chinese and the Indians also made their months start with the new moon. The early Egyptians started each month (inconveniently, it seems to me) on the last day on which the old moon was visible, but later on they divided their 365-day year into twelve named periods of 30 days each plus 5 extra days.

TIMING THE MOON

TO HAVE ANY CHANCE of predicting new moons we need to know the average length of the month – the interval between new moons or between full moons.

By 'new moon' here I mean the instant when the moon has the same longitude as the sun, not the first visible crescent as in the saying 'turn your money over when you see the new moon'. The astronomical new moon cannot be seen, so it is not easy to find the interval between new moons.

The moon remains full – that is to say, it is a circle as far as the eye can judge – for some while. But we can find the time of full moon to within half a day fairly easily. Because the full moon is opposite the sun it rises at sunset and sets at sunrise. And the moon rises or sets just under an hour later each day. If we watch the moon each day as it grows from half to full at a place with a flat horizon we can, with a little experience, pick out the last day on which the moon rises before sunset. The next day it rises after sunset, and the full moon is between these two sunsets. If we watch sunrises, we can pin the full moon down to an interval between two sunrises. If we do both, we can pin the full moon down to within half a day. We find the length of the month by dividing the interval between two full moons by the number of months between them. (This gives the average length of these particular months.)

There is no record of the Chinese, Babylonians or Greeks using this technique, nor any report of primitive tribes using it, although it is a pretty obvious one. However, the early Vedic astronomers in India are known to have used it, perhaps about 1000 BC.

THE MOTION OF THE MOON

STARTING PROBABLY somewhere before 250 BC, the Babylonians analyzed the motion of the moon in detail. A typical Babylonian tablet has data for full moons on the front and for new moons on the back.

The front of the tablet starts with the number of the year. The first column consists of the names of the months in order plus the name of the first month (of the next year). For each month there is a longitude: the longitude of the full moon in that month. This is exactly six signs from the longitude of the sun, which is calculated according to system A in some tablets, system B in others.

For each month the length of daylight on the day of the full moon is recorded; it is computed from the longitude of the sun.

A later column gives the latitude of the moon. Because the latitude is small the Babylonians used a small unit to measure it: the *she* (literally 'barley-corn'). Anyone who thinks it odd to use different units for measurements in different directions should reflect that for centuries the Royal Navy measured horizontal distances in cables and vertical distances in fathoms.

To the Babylonians the ecliptic was the centre-line of the band of positions in the sky occupied by the moon as it moved. They recognised it as the apparent path of the sun and knew that only when the moon is on or very near it is an eclipse possible. From the figures in the Babylonian tablets we can deduce their theory for the motion of the moon. Imagine a point, which I will call a *node*, moving westward along the ecliptic at a fixed rate (in fact just over 1½° per month). The moon moves eastward at a much faster rate, covering 360° in just over 27 days. When the moon is at the node its latitude is zero. As it moves its latitude increases by 1° for every 9° increase in longitude between it and the node until the latitude reaches 2°. It then increases at half that rate until it reaches 6°, decreases at this halved rate until it reaches 2° and then decreases at the original rate until it reaches zero. It then does the same thing on the other side of the ecliptic. You can easily calculate that in the complete cycle the moon has gained 360° of longitude over the node and so is back at the node again.

The point in the middle of the cycle where the latitude is zero is also called a node, and the westward motion is called the *regression of the nodes.* The time for the moon to go through a complete cycle is called a *latitudinal period.* It is a little over 27 days. The time for the moon to go from the ecliptic back to the ecliptic is half of this. If a full moon is near enough to the ecliptic it will be eclipsed. The nearer the ecliptic the larger the portion overshadowed, i.e. the larger the magnitude of the eclipse. The tablets recorded the computed magnitudes, and modern calculations show that they were reasonably accurate.

The next column in the tablet gives the change in the moon's longitude from one day to the next. This daily change increases at a constant rate to a maximum, decreases at the same rate to a minimum, increases to the maximum again, and so on. The time for a complete cycle is called the *period of anomaly* of the moon. ('Anomaly' here denotes a departure from regularity. See figure 30, page 61)

The computations underlying the Babylonian figures are remarkably sophisticated. The Babylonians discovered that 223 months, 242 latitudinal periods, and 239 periods of anomaly are each almost exactly equal to 6,585⅓ days. This means that if there is a total eclipse of the moon on one day then 6,585 days later (but eight hours later in the day) it is highly likely that there will be another, because a whole number of months have elapsed, so the moon will be full again, and a whole number of latitudinal periods have elapsed, so the moon will be back on the ecliptic. This computation is from averages, but because a whole number of periods of anomaly have elapsed the irregularities in the moon's motion over the whole period will pretty well even out.

To obtain these figures the Babylonians needed to know both the time interval between full moons and the longitude of the moon when full. The method described on page 57 is not accurate enough, but it is easy to judge quite accurately the middle of an eclipse of the moon, and that is the instant of new moon. And the theory of the sun's motion will give the longitude then. The further apart two eclipses are, the smaller the error when we divide the interval between them by the number of months. The time-interval mentioned above – 223 months – is long enough to give reasonable results and short enough to be practical. We do not know what, if anything, the Babylonians called this period, but modern astronomers call it a *saros.*

If we know the motion of the moon we can calculate the length of any particular saros. The Babylonians reversed this. From the variation in the length of the saros they deduced the variation in the moon's motion. The evidence that they used the saros is that in each tablet using system A the second column, right after the column of dates, is a column giving the excess over 6,585 days of the saros which starts at the relevant month.

The figures in the tablets are not raw observations; they are much too regular for that. The Babylonians deduced a maximum, a minimum, and a period from their observations and devised a scheme in which the saros increased at a constant rate from minimum to maximum, then decreased at the same rate, and so on. It is their regularity that enabled us to deduce the maximum and minimum, which do not appear explicitly in the tablets, because they are attained between full moons. Tablets have been found describing how to deduce the motion of the moon from the length of the saros.

The daily motion is used to compute the data in later columns: the exact length of the previous month and the time from sunset to the instant of full moon. Some tablets also list the times of moonrise and moonset.

TABLES OF ECLIPSES

THE ENTRIES which record the magnitude of an eclipse occur at five-month or six-month intervals. There is a good reason for this. Suppose that at a certain instant the moon is full and is bang on the ecliptic. It will be well and truly eclipsed. About 29½ days later it will again be full. But just over 27 days (one latitudinal period) after the first instant it will be back on the ecliptic, so by the time it is full it has had two days to move away from the ecliptic. This will take it too far away for an eclipse to be possible. Next month it will be even further away, but eventually it will reach its furthest distance away and will begin to return. On average, six months amount to 177 days and thirteen latitudinal half-periods to 176.7 days, so six months after a high-magnitude eclipse the full moon will be near the ecliptic and another eclipse is likely. How about five months? Five months average 147½ days and eleven latitudinal half-periods average 149½ days: not close enough. But these are average figures. Because the length of the month varies there can occasionally be an eclipse five months after another.

There is a Babylonian tablet that shows this quite strikingly. The first column gives the number of a year followed by the name of a month. Each entry is either five or six months after the previous one. Each column contains 38 entries and the intervals between them follow the same sequence of sixes and fives repeated over and over again. Another tablet some two hundred years later continues the same sequence and presumably tablets that we have not found fill the gap.

Each column covers 223 months, which is the length of the saros, so if we read across the table each entry is a saros after the previous one. Clearly the Babylonians had recognized a repeat-pattern for eclipses.

What would such a tablet be used for? The tablet shows only dates, no explanations. One possibility is that it is an eclipse-warning table. Once people discovered that eclipses of the sun take place only at new moon, then at least they know that on other nights there cannot be an eclipse; on a night of a new moon there might or might not be one visible at Babylon. When astronomers got a grip on the latitude of the moon they could rule out many new moons. In this tablet, each column, covering 223 months, contains only 38 days on which an eclipse can occur, therefore eliminating 185 false alarms.

Very similar five- and six-month intervals crop up in an entirely different part of the world: in central America, among the Mayas. The Dresden Codex contains the pages shown in figure 29. They are numbered 51 to 58 in the modern edition. Ignore the last half of page 58, to the right of the division down the middle; it starts a different topic.

Each page is divided into a top half and a bottom half. The first two half-pages, the tops of pages 51 and 52, are an introduction. The table itself starts at the top of page 53, followed by the other tops in order and then the bottom halves. I have numbered the columns of the table.

Each numbered column has a definite pattern: (A) two Mayan glyphs; (B) two or three combinations of shells, dots and bars, which are Mayan numerals; (C) three numeral-and-glyph combinations, which I shall explain later; and (D) two more numerals. After column 3 comes a wide column which is not part of the table and which I have not numbered. It consists of ten glyphs over a large picture. Nine such pictures occur at irregular intervals in the table.

The numbers (D) along the bottoms of the half-pages are all 177 or 148. The number of days in six months average 177 (to the nearest whole day) and the number of days in five months average 148. Clearly this table is analogous in some way to the Babylonian eclipse-warning table. The number before each of the large pictures is 148; the others are all 177.

The numbers (B) are a running total, each is obtained by adding the number (D) at the bottom of the column to the previous running total. However, there are six instances where 178 is added though 177 is shown. We shall see that these are not mistakes in addition; they are deliberate.

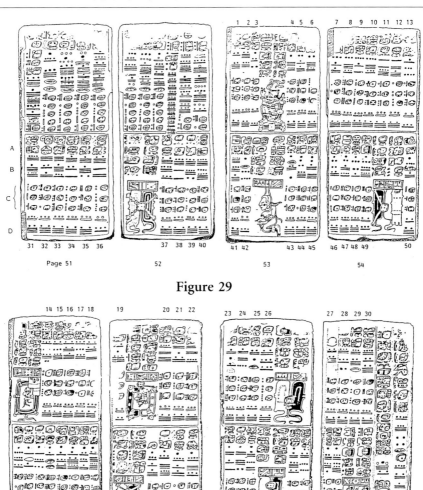

Figure 29

The table has 69 columns and divides neatly into three, with 23 columns in each third. In the first and second thirds the 148s occur in columns 3, 13 and 19 (of the 23); in the last third they occur in positions 3, 12 and 19, so the Mayan table, unlike the Babylonian ones, is not perfectly regular.

Each third of the table covers 135 months and 3,986 days. It looks as though the Mayas discovered that 135 months total 3,986 days and based their table on this relation. If so, their month is about seven minutes too short.

One way to find this figure would be to count the days between eclipses 135 months apart. Such pairs of eclipses are quite common, because 135 months is very close to a whole number of latitudinal half-periods. (The early Chinese also used this figure to try to predict eclipses.)

The Mayan astronomers had to produce a table covering 135 months, made up of five-month and six-month intervals, with substantially more of the latter. There is only one possible combination: 20 six-month intervals and 3 five-month intervals. This accounts for the fact that each third of the table contains 23 columns. However, the total number of days in 20 intervals of 177 days and 3 intervals of 148 days is 3,984 days – two days short. So twice in each third of the table an extra day has to be slipped in. It looks as though whoever compiled the table slipped in the extra days without telling the scribe who painted the codex and innocently filled in the 177s along the bottom without checking the addition.

The numeral-and-glyph combinations in the rows marked C in figure 29 are the Mayan 'sacred round'. This is a cycle of 260 days that is repeated over and over again, independently of the calendar, just as our cycle of the seven days of the week is repeated independently of the date.

The numbers in rows C have the same intervals between them as do the running totals. Where an extra 1 is added to the running total, the same happens to the sacred-round numbers, which confirms that this is deliberate. In each column the day in the top row C is one day earlier than the day in the middle row, which is one day earlier than the day in the bottom row.

We do not know for certain why the Mayas chose 260 days for the length of the sacred round, but the Mayas still living in Momostenango, who still use the sacred round to determine the dates of rituals and for divination, say that it is the length of the ideal human pregnancy, in which a baby is born on the same day of the round as it was conceived. (And, of course, gestation does take about 260 days.) It is also the ideal interval between planting and reaping maize.

There is a neat tie-in between the length of the sacred round and intervals between eclipses. As a result of the motion of the sun and the nodes the sun takes just over 173 days to go from one node to the next. Three of these intervals add up to 520 days: just twice a sacred round. So the days on which the sun is near a node cluster in three equally-spaced sectors of the sacred round. Only on these days can an eclipse occur. And the sacred-round dates in the table do cluster in three sectors.

How might the Mayas, without any theory of the motion of the moon, have hit on the idea that a table for eclipses should be built up from five-month and six-month intervals? Possibly by counting the numbers of months between the eclipses that they observed.

Between AD 400 and 500 seventy-three eclipses of the moon were visible in the Mayan region. By far the commonest interval between successive eclipses was six months. The only other intervals that occurred were of 11, 12, 17, 18, 23, 29, 35, 41, 53, 59, and 65 months. Each of these can be made up of six-month intervals, with or without one five-month interval. For example, 23 = 6+6+6+5. This could easily give rise to the idea that a table for eclipses should be based on five-month and six-month intervals, with substantially more of six months than of five.

HOW LONG IS THE MONTH?

A BABYLONIAN TABLET dated about 100 BC gives the lengths of the months in days and fractions of a day. If plotted on a graph, as shown in figure 30 they lie on a zig-zag, and it is easy to compute the maximum and minimum values, i.e. the values given by the points A and B. Converted to decimals they are 29.75 and 29.31 days, to two places of decimals. Modern estimates for the maximum and minimum length of a month are 29.80 and 29.27 days.

For long-term calculations the average length of a month is important. Because the Babylonian values lie on a zig-zag the average value is half-way between the minimum and the maximum. In sexagesimals it is 29, 31, 50, 08, 20 days.

The Greek astronomer Hipparchus, about 150 BC, used exactly the same value. It is beyond coincidence that exactly these numbers could have been found twice independently. The two civilizations were in close contact after the conquest of the middle east by Alexander the Great in 334 BC and either of the civilizations could have got these figures from the other. They agree to the nearest second with figures given in modern almanacs.

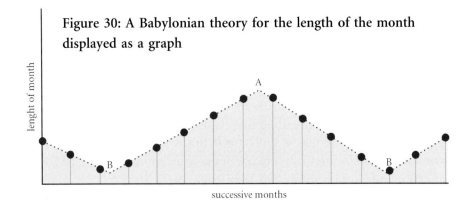

Figure 30: A Babylonian theory for the length of the month displayed as a graph

lenght of month

successive months

Ptolemy also quoted Hipparchus as having 4,267 months equal to 126,007 days plus one hour, but this does not yield quite the same result.

The Indian astronomer Aryabhata had a value for the average length of the month about 2 seconds too short.

As mentioned on page 13, the Chinese had estimates for the length of the month. The *Zhou bi* gives a length calculated from the number of days in a year and the relation 19 years = 235 months. This estimate is about 22 seconds too long. As time passed the Chinese improved on this, and the *Shou shi* almanac, just before AD 1300, gave (in decimals) a month about one-third of a second too long. The Chinese have left no description of how they found this excellent figure.

The Mayas also had estimates for the length of the month. How do we know this? A typical Mayan inscription, recording perhaps the birth, death or accession of a ruler, or an important rite, gives the date of the event and very often the number of days since the last new moon. It also gives the number of the new moon (new moons were numbered in sixes) and states whether the previous new moon was 29 or 30 days earlier. Some of these dates are mythical, being the dates of birth of gods some two or three thousand years ago. So the figures for the moon on these dates must be calculated, not deduced from observations. Starting from one basic date, which may have been based on observation, the Mayas could calculate the figures for any other date from a relation between months and days. From the figures on the inscriptions, historians have deduced the relations that the Mayas probably used: at Palenque 81 months = 2,392 days (giving a month 24 seconds too long); at Copan 149 months = 4,400 days (33 seconds too short). Both estimates are much better than the one that seems to underlie the Dresden Codex.

GREEK AND INDIAN THEORIES

EUDOXUS MODELLED the motion of the moon in much the same way as the sun, using three interconnected spheres. The outermost sphere rotated once a day about the pole-to-pole axis and, by reproducing the daily rotation of the sky, accounted for the moon's rising and setting. The next sphere rotated about an axis inclined to the pole-to-pole axis at an angle equal to the angle between the ecliptic and the equator. It reproduced the progress of the moon along the ecliptic. The rotation would have to take just less than a month, because in a month the moon has to go completely round the ecliptic and a bit more to catch up with the sun.

The third sphere rotated slowly about an axis inclined at a small angle to the axis of the second sphere. It accounted for the deviation of the moon from the ecliptic, including the fact that the greatest deviation does not always occur at the same place on the ecliptic, but at a point that moves steadily westward. The points of greatest deviation move at the same rate as the points of no deviation, the nodes, so this third sphere accounted for the regression of the nodes.

As it stands this is not very good. The moon would spend just over 9 years each side of the ecliptic, whereas in fact it crosses it every month. If Eudoxus had made the second sphere rotate at the rate of regression of the nodes and the third sphere rotate once in just under a month, all would have been well. Perhaps this is what Eudoxus did and the description that has come down to us is mistaken.

Hipparchus's theory of the motion of the moon was something like his theory of the motion of the sun. As shown in figure 31, a point C moves in a circle round the earth T just fast enough to complete a revolution in the average length of a month. It carries a small circle called an *epicycle*. The moon L moves round the ecliptic with a period equal to the time for the speed of the moon along the ecliptic to vary from its greatest value to its least value and back again. This period (the period of anomaly) was known to the Babylonians.

This theory was devised in order to give the right variation in the speed of the moon round the ecliptic, but as a by-product it determines the shape of the moon's orbit. In particular, it determines the ratio of the greatest distance of the moon to its least distance. Hipparchus had two shots at the relative sizes of his two circles. Both made the ratio of the greatest distance to the least distance a little too big.

Ptolemy found that Hipparchus's theory gave reasonably accurate results at full moon and new moon – not surprising, as it was based on observations of eclipses – but was not so accurate in between. So he modified it. Unfortunately his modification gave quite a wrong shape to the orbit and made the moon's greatest

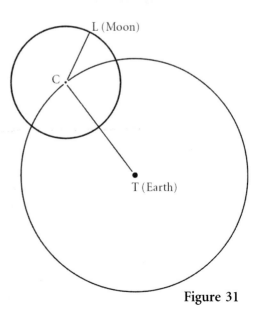

Figure 31

distance nearly twice its least distance, which any moon-watcher can see is not so.

Later the Arabs replaced Ptolemy's modification by one which had the same effect on the moon's speed without distorting its orbit. Brahe and Kepler made further improvements. Modern astronomers have given up geometrical models and compute the position of the moon from a complicated formula (which can be found in the explanatory supplement to the Nautical Almanac).

The Indian theory of the motion of the moon was like Hipparchus's and was therefore inaccurate between new and full moons. This did not prevent the Indians from predicting eclipses, which happen only at new and full moon. This ability became newsworthy in 1850 when an English officer found in Pondicherry a calendar-maker who successfully predicted an eclipse using seashells laid out in a pattern on the ground to represent numbers.

HOW FAR AWAY IS THE MOON?

WHEN WE COME to methods for finding the distance of the moon from the earth we need to know, for the first time, that the earth is a sphere and how big it is. The Chinese, the Babylonians and the Mayas did not, as far as we know, try to find the distance of the moon. The Greeks did.

The Greek theory of the motion of the moon gives the direction of the moon from the centre, T, of the earth. Observation gives the direction of the moon from an observer on the surface of the earth. From these two directions we can find the proportions of the triangle formed by the moon, the observer, and T.

Ptolemy estimated the average distance of the moon as 49 times the radius of the earth. The correct figure is 60.

NODES AND ECLIPSES

AS THE MOON MOVES round its orbit it deviates from the ecliptic. (Both the Babylonian tablets and Eudoxus's model recognized this.) The easiest way to visualize this is to project the orbits of the sun and moon onto the celestial sphere. (This is what a planetarium does, except that the dome represents only half of the sphere.)

The sun's orbit – the ecliptic – is a great circle on this sphere (i.e. a circle whose centre is the centre of the sphere). The moon's orbit is another great circle, intersecting the ecliptic at the two nodes. The nodes are moving slowly (regressing) round the ecliptic, taking just under 19 years to make a complete circuit. The angle between the two orbits is called the *inclination* and is about 5°. It is almost constant; it varies by only one-third of a degree.

About every 9½ years the nodes will be at the equinox-points on the ecliptic; this is the time for the nodes to make half a circuit, from one equinox point to the other. When this happens, a full or new moon near the time of the equinox will be near the ecliptic and an eclipse will be likely.

Near the time of a solstice, with the sun and the moon half-way between the points where the orbits intersect, the moon is well away (by about 5°) from the ecliptic and an eclipse is impossible. To sum up: in these years eclipses are likely in spring and autumn, not in summer and winter.

Halfway between these years the nodes are at the solstice points. Now eclipses are likely near the solstices, impossible near the equinoxes.

The angle between the celestial equator and the ecliptic is the obliquity. These two great circles intersect at the equinox points. So when the nodes are at the equinox points the ecliptic, the equator, and the moon's orbit all intersect in these two points. Then the angle between the moon's orbit and the equator is either the obliquity plus the inclination or the obliquity minus the inclination; about every 19 years it will be one, halfway between these times it will be the other. These are the greatest and least angles between the moon's orbit and the equator. We will soon see the importance of this.

WHERE DOES THE MOON RISE?

DID EARLY PEOPLE watch the positions at which the moon rose and set, as they did for the sun?

The progress of the moon along the horizon is vastly more complicated than the progress of the sun. Sunrise moves steadily and gradually, at most ½° at a time. But moonrise may change by over 10° from one day to the next. The moon can rise at any time of the day or night, and when it rises in broad daylight you can't see it. Nor can you see it at new moon, or for a day or two before or after. Anthropologists have found plenty of people who tracked the sun along the horizon, but no-one who tracked the moon.

There is another complication. Every 19 or so years the orbit of the moon makes a greater angle with the ecliptic than does the orbit of the sun. Then the swing of moonrise along the horizon is greater than the swing of sunrise, and the moon can rise further north than the sun ever rises. About 9 years later, the swing of moonrise will be less than the swing of sunrise. Halfway between these two dates the swings are equal.

(All these considerations apply equally well to the setting moon.)

In spite of these snags it looks as though people were interested in the most northerly moonrise at Stonehenge. The heel-stone, when seen from the centre, marks the most northerly sunrise. To the left of the heel-stone are some rows of post-holes, which suggest that someone was watching something on the horizon just north of the most northerly sunrise. They cover an arc of about 10°, and this is just the difference between the most northerly moonrise and sunrise at the latitude of Stonehenge. And there is a stone, marked D in figure 1 (on page 4), which marks the most northerly moonrise when viewed from the centre.

The people who built Stonehenge may well have felt that there was some natural or supernatural law that prevented the sun from rising outside certain limits on the horizon, and this law usually applied also to the moon. But just occasionally the moon broke the taboo.

There is further evidence. Stonehenge is essentially a circular construction with an axis. Why would the builders incorporate a rectangle: stones 91, 92, 93 and 94? Archaeologists have not suggested a reason, but astronomers have. If the people at Stonehenge were investigating the most northerly moonrise they would have found that the angle between it and the most southerly sunrise is a right angle. This is the same as the angle between the most northerly sunrise and the most southerly moonrise. If the astronomers knew or guessed this fact they would see that a line at right angles to the main axis of Stonehenge (which points to the most northerly sunrise) would point to the most southerly moonrise. And that is just what the long sides of the rectangle do.

Perhaps the astronomers at Stonehenge did something a good deal more subtle than this – perhaps they marked the most northerly and southerly moonrises at the time when the swing is least. They would have to do more than just watch the positions of moonrise and note the extremes; they would have to realize that the swing from one extreme to the other varies in extent and that this variation is regular in a cycle of just under nineteen years. They must then mark the extremes at the right time in the cycle.

What is the evidence for this? A rectangle can have any proportions – short and fat or long and thin – so even if the directions of the sides are fixed, the diagonals can point in any desired direction. One of the diagonals, from stone 93 to stone 91, does point within three degrees of the southernmost moonrise when the swing is least. And on the other side of the entrance from stone D is stone F, situated in the right place to mark the northernmost moonrise when the swing is least.

Anyone who discovered this cycle would have some information about eclipses, because when the swing is greatest or least eclipses are likely in the middle of spring and autumn and impossible in the middle of summer or winter. Midway between the times of greatest and least swing eclipses are likely in summer and winter and impossible in the middle of spring or autumn.

PREDICTING ECLIPSES

EVEN WITH MUCH LESS sophistication than this it is possible to make some predictions about eclipses. We watch the moonrise at sunset on the day closest to full moon. We can tell, by seeing whether the shadow of a post at sunset points to the place where the moon rises, whether the moon rises directly opposite the sun or not. If it does, it must be on the ecliptic and there will be an eclipse.

Eclipses of the moon happen more often that most people think. It is total eclipses that get reported in newspapers, and they are fairly rare, but a partial eclipse is easily visible to anyone who is interested enough to look for it. The shadow of the earth takes quite a definite sharp-edged bite out of the moon. Partial eclipses that take place in day-time cannot be seen. But those that can be seen happen often enough for people to be able to detect some regularity.

We have seen that six months after an eclipse there is a fair chance of another, and that 223 months after an eclipse there is a good chance of another. The way that the Babylonians arranged their tables showed that they knew this. Whenever a whole number of months is equal to a whole number of node-to-node intervals, we have a good eclipse interval. For instance, 135 average months differ from 293 average node-to-node intervals by less than an hour. In 7 BC, Lin Xiu used this interval in his *San Tong* almanac, and perhaps it is no coincidence that 135 months is the length of each third of the Mayan eclipse table.

Whether these intervals could be used to predict eclipses is a moot point. If they could, people who were not able to compute the latitude and longitude of the moon could predict eclipses by counting days. However, we have no record of anyone doing this successfully.

The first known record anywhere in the world of an eclipse being successfully predicted, followed by a record of its being observed, is in a Babylonian source of 612 BC.

By AD 206 the *Qian Xing* almanac contained details of the latitude and longitude of the moon, so from then on the Chinese had a way to predict eclipses. They were eventually able to predict the times of eclipses to within an hour or so.

ECLIPSES OF THE SUN

ECLIPSES OF THE SUN are a very different kettle of fish from eclipses of the moon. For one thing, they are much more spectacular – at least, total eclipses are. But a partial eclipse of the sun, in which from your point of view the sun is only partly covered by the moon, is not. If a partial eclipse takes place in the middle of the day it may well not be noticed. Unless it is very nearly total the sunlight will not be noticeably dimmed, and unless there is a light transparent cloud cover no-one will be looking at the sun; it would be too painful. And if it takes place near dawn or dusk it will not be remarkable. I was once walking on the beach when there was a partial eclipse of the sun just before sunset. Although I could see quite clearly the moon taking a bite out of the sun, which was much too hard-edged and accurately circular to be caused by a cloud, no-one else was taking the slightest notice.

Popular writers on astronomy are fond of saying that eclipses of the sun are, surprisingly, more common than eclipses of the moon. This is because almanacs such as Oppolzer's famous *Canon of eclipses* record an eclipse whenever the shadow of the moon covers any part of the earth. Clearly this was meaningless to people, like the Babylonians and the Mayas, who had no idea of the size and shape of the earth. What mattered to them was eclipses that they could see: only three total eclipses were visible in Mayan territories between AD 100 and AD 1000. Eclipses visible at any one place are rare.

This is because the shadow of the moon on the earth is tiny and the strip of earth that it covers is very narrow. In fact, the shadow may not even reach the earth. When this happens, if the moon passes across the middle of the sun, it leaves a bright ring round the edge uncovered. This is an *annular* eclipse. Annular eclipses, of course, furnish strong evidence that either the distance of the moon or the distance of the sun or both must vary.

However, once, people began to get a good idea of the movements of the sun and moon, especially of the way in which the moon deviates from the ecliptic, they could tell when an eclipse of the sun is likely and when it is impossible. The Babylonians could do this, though there is no record of a successful prediction. The later Greeks, the Indians, the Arabs, and the later Chinese could do it fairly well.

4

The Planets

VENUS

V ENUS IS THE BRIGHTEST PLANET. If we watch it over a long period we find the same appearances repeating over and over again.

One morning Venus rises just before the sun and can be seen for a short while before it is swamped by sunlight. As the days pass the apparent distance between Venus and the sun increases, reaches a maximum, and then decreases until Venus is too close to the sun to be seen. This part of the cycle of appearances – Venus as morning star – takes 263 days on average but can vary by several days.

Venus remains invisible for about 50 days and then begins to appear in the evening, setting just after sunset. Its apparent distance from the sun increases and then decreases until it is too close to the sun to be seen. This period – Venus as evening star – lasts, like the morning period, about 263 days. Venus then remains invisible for a period that varies from 1 day to 20 days, and then appears in the morning and the cycle starts again.

The whole cycle takes between 575 and 590 days. The technical name for the length of the cycle is the *synodic period* of Venus.

The very early Greeks thought that Venus was two planets, *Eosphoros* in the morning and *Hesperus* in the evening, but by about 500 BC they knew that there was only one Venus, which they called *Aphrodite*.

The Incas knew that the morning star and evening star were the same. They thought that the sun, as lord of all the stars, ordered Venus to keep near him, sometimes in front and sometimes behind, because she was more beautiful than the other stars.

The Mayas were interested in Venus, as we can see from five pages of the Dresden Codex. The right-hand half of each page consists of pictures and text concerned with mythological omens. It is the left hand halves that interest astronomers. These are reproduced as figure 32.

Along the bottom of each half-page are the Mayan numerals for 236, 90, 250 and 8. (The numeral for 236 was miscopied; one bar is missing.) These

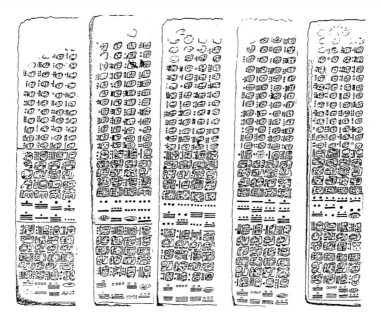

Figure 32

numbers add up to 584, the average number of days in the synodic period of Venus to the nearest whole day. The individual numbers give roughly the periods of visibility and invisibility – very roughly: the 90 is almost twice what it should be.

Why is the table so impossibly regular? In particular, why is the short period of invisibility always allotted 8 days when in fact it varies from one day to 20? Perhaps the table does not represent the appearances of Venus itself but of a theoretical body that is based on Venus but moves more regularly. This would be analogous to our 'ecclesiastical new moon' used to determine the date of Easter, or to the Greeks' 'mean sun'.

The Mayas used the cycle of Venus to set the dates of such things as accessions to the throne, ritual sacrifices, or even attacks on neighbouring cities. Some inscriptions (on lintels, panels and stelas) show a particular type of costume that Mayanists call a Venus/Tlaloc costume. (Tlaloc is the Mayas' rain-god.) An unexpectedly high proportion of dates in these inscriptions are close to a date of a first appearance of Venus in the evening. And a rather high proportion of them are close to dates at which the height of Venus in the sky is at a maximum. (The height at which Venus is visible is restricted because Venus is never more than 47° from the sun and not visible unless the sun is below, or very close to, the horizon.)

To us, new year's day is a special occasion. If the number of the *tun* (see appendix 2 page 105) ended in zero it would be analogous to our decade (and would be twice as special, as it comes round only half as often). Eight such dates have been found in inscriptions displaying Venus/Tlaloc costumes. Four of these are near to maximum elevations of Venus. The other four are close to first appearances of Venus in the evening, and these four follow a definite progression. They are respectively 14 days after, 4 days after, 4 days before and 10 days before an actual first appearance. The dates have obviously been computed from an estimate of the synodic period that is a trifle too short. The other four follow a less definite progression. This is not surprising; a maximum elevation is much harder for the eye to judge accurately than a first appearance.

The Chinese tracked the planet completely round the ecliptic, giving time-intervals and differences in longitude. The *Si fen* almanac of just after AD 100 gave the following figures.

days	91	91	46	8	10	10	10	8	46	91	91	82+562/23,320
degrees	113	106	33	0	-6	-8	-6	0	33	106	113	100+

The table starts when Venus first appears in the evening. In the first 91 days it covers 113 degrees. A Chinese degree is the average distance that the sun covers in a day (there are 365¼ of them to a complete circle) so we can see Venus gaining on the sun. Then it slows down slightly, covering only 106 degrees in the next 91 days. Presumably the interval of 91 days was chosen because it is a quarter of a year, to the nearest whole day. Venus then slows down drastically – only 33 degrees in 46 days – remains stationary for 8 days, and slips back by 6 degrees in 10 days. By now it has covered 246 degrees in 246 days, so it is back where it started relative to the sun, and on the verge of becoming invisible. It stays invisible for 10 days, slipping back 8 degrees, so it is now on the other side of the sun and becomes visible in the morning. The motion now repeats itself symmetrically until the last column but one, when Venus makes its last appearance in the morning. It now becomes invisible for a tad over 82 days. The reason for the gargantuan fraction is that the Chinese had an estimate that 2,915 synodic periods take 4,661 years. They computed the period in days exactly at 365¼ days to the year and put in the fraction to give the correct total.

MERCURY

MERCURY behaves like Venus but being dimmer and closer to the sun (never more than 27° away) it is much harder to see.

The Chinese, the Indians and the earlier Greeks treated Mercury like

Venus. We have no evidence that the Mayas took any notice of Mercury at all.

JUPITER

LIKE VENUS and Mercury, Jupiter moves close to the ecliptic, but unlike them it is not constrained to be near the sun. So what we see is quite different.

One morning Jupiter rises just before the sun, and is visible until sunrise. It travels eastward but a little slower than the sun, so its angular distance from the sun increases. Each successive morning it rises a little earlier and is visible for longer. Eventually it is visible the whole night, rising at sunset. It is now at the point of the ecliptic opposite the sun – it is said to be in opposition. The eastward motion slows, stops, reverses, stops again and reverses again, continuing in its original eastward direction. Soon Jupiter begins to rise after sunset and so is visible only late at night. As it rises later and later the period during which it is visible grows shorter and shorter until it is no longer visible. After a while the whole cycle is repeated. The westward motion is *retrogression*.

This motion is shown quite clearly by a table in the *Si fen* almanac, like the one that I quoted for Venus.

MARS AND SATURN

MARS AND SATURN behave like Jupiter. The Chinese, the Indians and the Greeks treated them both like Jupiter. The Mayas may possibly have watched Mars; there is a table in the Dresden Codex which spans 780 days (three sacred rounds) and this is the synodic period of Mars.

THE BABYLONIANS

THE BABYLONIANS showed interest in Venus very early on, probably about 1700 to 1600 BC. The *Venus tablets of Ammisaduqa* recorded appearances and disappearances, with astrological comments. For example, one omen said that on the 15th of Shabati Venus disappeared. It reappeared on the 18th. Springs will open, Adad will bring rain, Ea will bring floods, and kings will send messages of reconciliation to each other. (Shabati is the 11th month of the Babylonian year; Adad and Ea are gods.)

From about 300 BC we have many detailed mathematical tablets. Each deals with one visible phenomenon for one planet. The visible phenomena for Venus or Mercury are its first and last appearance in the morning and evening (as explained on page 72 for Venus) and the beginning and end of westward motion with respect to the stars. For the other three planets the phenomena are the first and last appearance, the opposition and the beginning and end of westward motion (as explained on page 75 for Jupiter).

One tablet for Mercury shows the calculated dates and longitudes of successive first appearances over a number of years. There is also an 'instruction tablet' that explains how to calculate the date and longitude of one appearance from the previous one. We have many tables of this sort for the planets, but only one giving the dated longitudes of a planet between the visible phenomena.

THE GREEKS USE GEOMETRY

THE ANCIENT GREEKS were excellent geometers; everyone knows about Euclid. Eudoxus, Archimedes, Apollonius and Ptolemy pushed geometry to even greater heights. We have seen that the Greeks applied geometry to the sun and the moon, but their real genius lay in their treatment of the planets.

The most remarkable thing about the outer planets, Saturn, Jupiter and Mars, is their retrogression. Tables, like the Chinese ones, which show motion along the ecliptic can exhibit the retrogression but cannot explain it. A geometrical theory might be able to.

In fact, Theon of Smyrna, in the second century AD, remarked that though the Babylonians could reproduce the various motions and even predict future phenomena, they did not afford an understanding, and we should also examine these things physically.

Eudoxus's model for the motion of Jupiter was ingenious. It explained not only the retrogression but also the fact that in the middle of retrogression Jupiter is opposite the sun. It also explained the deviation of Jupiter from the ecliptic; in fact, the descriptions that have come down to us from Aristotle and Simplicius mention this deviation but not the retrogression.

Eudoxus ingeniously linked two spheres together in such a way that their combined motion made a point on one of them move around a figure-of-eight. He then placed these spheres inside a pair of spheres arranged like the ones that he used for the sun, shown in figure 16 earlier. This made the figure-of-eight move round the ecliptic, as shown in

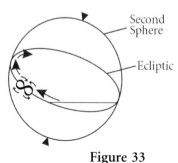

Figure 33

figure 33. About half of the time Jupiter is moving backwards on the figure-of-eight faster than the figure-of-eight is moving forwards; this produces the retrogression.

The model has some serious flaws. If we choose the details to give the right amount of retrogression, i.e. the right length of the figure-of-eight, it turns out that this fixes the breadth of the figure-of-eight, which in turn determines the greatest deviation from the ecliptic, and gives it the wrong value. The model also makes Jupiter cross the ecliptic four times in every synodic period; it doesn't do this. And it has Jupiter on the ecliptic at every opposition; in fact it isn't.

Mars and Saturn behave like Jupiter, and Eudoxus treated them in the same way.

To sum up: the model is mathematically ingenious but astronomically unsound. But it is important. It is almost certainly this model that inspired the later Greeks to apply geometry to astronomy, something that the Babylonians and the Mayas never thought of doing. The Indians, Arabs and later European astronomers based their models on the Greek ones.

To a watcher of the skies, Venus and Mercury behave very differently from the other planets. But it must at some time have struck a thoughtful astronomer that the change from evening star to morning star is in fact a retrogression: Venus and Mercury retrogress past the sun. So Eudoxus could use the same model for them. The objections mentioned earlier still apply and there is one more: Eudoxus's model makes the period of invisibility between morning star and evening star equal to the period between evening star and morning star, whereas for Venus the first period is about fifty days and the second varies from one day to twenty days.

The later Greek theory of the motion of the planets was quite different. It probably started fairly simply. A point called the *mean planet* moves in a circle called the *deferent* round the earth in the plane of the ecliptic. The planet itself moves in a small circle called an *epicycle* round the mean planet in the same direction (anticlockwise in my diagrams). Figure 34 shows this. The motion round the epicycle produces retrogression, and a slight tilting of the epicycle produces the small deviations of the planet from the ecliptic.

The model was only a scale model. The theory involved only ratios: for example, the ratio of the size of the epicycle to the size of the deferent. Not until very late did the Greeks try to find actual distances. (And, as we shall see, unsuccessfully.)

For Venus and Mercury, which revolve round the sun, the mean planet should be the sun, but because the model is only a scale model we can say only that the mean planet is in the same direction as the sun from the earth. Probably because of their fixation on regular motion, the Greeks aligned the mean planet on the mean sun, not on the sun itself. The mean sun is an imaginary body moving round the ecliptic whose direction from the earth is parallel to the line CS in figure 17 on page 29, so that it moves at constant speed.

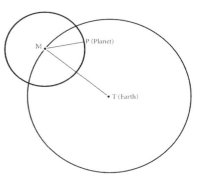

Figure 34: An early Greek theory for the motion of a planet

The planet moves round the epicycle once in a synodic period: if at any instant it is on the line joining the earth to the mean planet, then one synodic period later it will be back on the line joining the earth to the (new position of the) mean planet.

For each of the outer planets – Mars, Jupiter and Saturn – the planet still circles the mean planet at one revolution per synodic period. The time taken for the mean planet to circle the earth is its sidereal period.

The rate of revolution in space of the line joining the mean planet to the planet is one revolution per year. So if at any time this line points towards the mean sun, it will always point to the mean sun. But it does point towards the mean sun in the middle of retrogression, which takes place when the planet P is directly between the mean planet M and the earth T, which happens when the planet is opposite the mean sun S. Then PT points towards S, so P, M, T and S are all in one straight line, and MP points towards S.

The epicycle was introduced into the theory of the moon's motion to account for its irregularity. As a by-product it fixed the shape of the orbit, but gave it quite the wrong shape. How about the planets?

For Venus, the answer is simple. Its actual motion relative to the earth, leaving aside small irregularities, is motion in a circle round a point (the sun) which itself moves in a circle round the earth. The Greeks had only to get the ratio of the sizes of the epicycle and the deferent equal to the ratio of the sizes of the orbits of Venus and the earth to have a good scale model.

The same applies, believe it or not, to the outer planets. But to see this needs some sophisticated geometry.

This model did not account for various small irregularities, so it had to be modified. The irregularities have two causes: the irregular motion of the earth and the irregular motion of the planet. This would correspond to irregular motion of the mean planet and irregular motion of the planet round it. However, Ptolemy kept the motion of the planet round the mean planet perfectly regular and tried to account for all the irregularities by tinkering with the motion of the mean planet. We find the final version of his theory in the *Syntaxis*.

THE INDIANS

THE INDIANS also used epicycles to model the motion of the planets, but they used them differently. Slightly different versions appeared over the years.

Let us start with Venus or Mercury. A point M moves round the earth T in such a way that the line TM points to the mean sun. In Sanskrit, M is called the *madhya graha: madhya* = middle, *graha* = planet. The planet itself is called *sphuta graha: sphuta* = evident. M carries two epicycles, as shown in figure 35. Round one of them called *sighra* (fast) a point P_s moves at a constant rate which we recognize today as the rate at which the planet revolves around the sun. (Describing the motion in this way suggests that the Indians had some inkling that Venus and Mercury revolve round the sun.)

M carries another, much smaller, epicycle called *manda* (slow). On it is a point P_m placed so that the line from H to P_m is in a fixed direction in space. Both epicycles vary in size as time passes.

The theory for the three outer planets is the same except that now M revolves round the earth in a period of its own and MP_s points to the mean sun.

The longitude of M and the directions of the lines from M to P_m and P_s at any given instant can be calculated. An early source said that the planet was pulled away from M with cords of wind by celestial demons at P_m and P_s. In fact, the longitude of the planet was found by algebraic calculation.

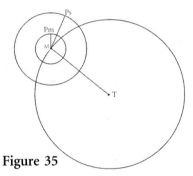

Figure 35

THE PATHS OF THE PLANETS

THE SHAPES of the paths of the planets – moving figures-of-eight for Eudoxus, epicycloids for Ptolemy, and complicated curves for Aryabhata – are only by-products of theories devised to give the right motion in longitude. There was no direct measurement of their actual shapes. The Chinese seem to have given little thought to the shapes of the orbits, though one writer did say that a planet's path had the shape of a willow leaf moving round the ecliptic.

5

The Earth

W hat happens if you start to walk or paddle and keep on moving in the same direction? Can you go on for ever, or will you eventually come to the 'ends of the earth' and have to stop? Very early people might not have thought about this. However, as soon as people realized that when the sun sets it is not destroyed, to be created anew next day, but somehow passes under the earth, they could see that the earth must come to an end somewhere.

If the earth is surrounded by empty space, the obvious question is what supports it? The Aztecs thought that it was on the back of a gigantic reptile. You may know the story of the naive person arguing with the professor of astronomy:

NP: The earth is supported by an enormous turtle.

P of A: What supports the turtle?

NP: Another turtle.

P of A: What supports the second turtle?

NP: A third turtle.

P of A: What supports ...

NP: It's no good, professor. It's turtles all the way down.

The Greeks did not appeal to animals for support. Thales thought that the earth floated on water. Anaximander said that it is necessarily at rest and does not need support. Aristotle thought that it was held at the centre of the universe by its natural tendency to be there. The later followers of Pythagoras thought that the earth circled round a central fire.

WHAT SHAPE IS THE EARTH?

What shape is the earth? Some parts of the Chinese *Zhou bi* implied that its surface is flat, other parts that it is heaped up in the middle. The *hun tian* theory implied, as far as we can tell, that the surface is flat, possibly the top of a body shaped roughly like a hemisphere. Anaximander thought that it is shaped like a drum whose diameter is three times its height; we live on one of the flat surfaces.

But everyone who gave serious thought to the question, rather than mere speculation, seems to have found that the earth is a sphere. The first person, as far as we know, to give reasons for this is Aristotle. Some of his reasons were good; some bad. Good: the shadow of the earth on the moon in an eclipse is convex with a circular edge, leaving a concave illuminated part, contrasting with the convex illuminated part of the non-eclipsed moon between half-moon and full moon. Also good: some stars which can be seen from Egypt cannot be seen from further north. Bad: the particles that make up the earth will converge into a sphere because the natural movement of the element earth is downward. Aristotle did not mention the fact that a ship a long way away appears unexpectedly low in the water: sailors call this 'being hull down on the horizon'. But, according to Strabo, Homer knew this, and Homer was long before Aristotle.

Why does the sun sink obliquely as it sets instead of sinking straight down? Why do stars do the same? For that matter, why do they set at all; why not revolve round the earth in horizontal circles? The fact that the earth is round explains this. If their orbits are horizontal to us they won't be horizontal to someone further round the earth, and there is no reason why we should be specially privileged.

The elevation of the pole above the horizon at any place is equal to the latitude of that place. Just as a modern gazetteer lists the latitude (and longitude) of each place, so Chinese almanacs listed the elevation of the pole at each place. From early times the Chinese knew that the further north the higher the pole. By just after AD 700 they knew precisely how the elevation varied with the position of the observer, as the result of measurements made at places on a north-to-south line stretching from the Great Wall to Indo-China. The change in elevation is exactly proportional to north-to-south distance: if you travel south you reduce the elevation, and if you travel twice as far south you reduce it by twice as much. This is precisely what must happen if the earth is a sphere, but the Chinese did not make the obvious deduction.

HOW BIG IS THE EARTH?

SO THE EARTH is round. How big is it? The earliest estimate that we know of was mentioned by Aristotle: the circumference is 400,000 stades. He was surprised at how small the earth is, but in fact this estimate is too large. We can't say just how much too large because the Greeks used several different stades and we do not know which one Aristotle was using.

How could we try to find the size of the earth? We could compare the local times of an eclipse observed at two places at the same known latitude a known distance apart. Arab astronomers, just after AD 900, did this at Baghdad and Mecca. Instead of an eclipse we could use the instant when the moon began to cover a particular star.

Alternatively we could find the angle by which the horizon falls below the horizontal when seen from the top of a mountain. The Arabs used this method but did not have a good estimate of the height of the mountain that they used – it is not easy to measure the height of a mountain. We could get over this snag by making an observation from the top of a vertical cliff, whose height we find by dropping a plumb-line to the sea halfway between high tide and low tide, but now we have to measure a very small angle, which is hard to do accurately. In either case, even if we get both the angle and the height correct our result will be about 20 per cent too high because of refraction.

A third method is to measure the difference between the elevations of the pole at two places, one due south of the other, a difference between two angles that are nearly equal, in which case the error is apt to be large. For example, if one angle is between 34.5° and 35.5° and the other between 36.5° and 37.5°, both reasonably precise estimates, the difference between them can be anywhere from 1° to 3°, and one value will yield a result three times as big as the other. On the other hand, if the two places are far apart it is hard to measure the distance between them accurately.

Equally well, we could measure the difference between the elevations of the sun at noon on the summer solstice at the two places. Eratosthenes used this method about 200 BC. He found that at noon on the summer solstice at Alexandria the sun was one-fiftieth of a revolution from the vertical. He had heard that at noon on the summer solstice the sun shone straight down a well at Syene, which is (very nearly) due south of Alexandria. This implies that the angle between the vertical directions at Alexandria and Syene is one-fiftieth of a revolution, so the circumference of the earth is fifty times the distance between them. Eratosthenes quoted a distance of 5,000 stades, which, if he used the most likely stade, gives a circumference 17 per cent too large.

There are some doubts about how valid Eratosthenes's estimate is. Where, for example, did he get the figure of 5,000 stades? It is not possible to pace out the straight line from Alexandria to Syene across the sands. The French astronomer Laplace suggested that Eratosthenes was unwittingly using an estimate of this distance derived from a previous estimate of the size of the earth.

The angle that Eratosthenes quoted, one-fiftieth of a revolution, is about a quarter of a degree too small. This is because he found the elevation of the sun by using a gnomon, which, as explained on page 15, makes the elevation of the sun a quarter of a degree too high.

THE MOTION OF THE EARTH

DOES THE EARTH MOVE? Common sense suggests that the solid earth on which we stand is fixed. Presumably most early people took this view, but the Greeks did raise the question.

The Pythagoreans, around 500 BC, thought that the earth moved round a fire in the middle of the universe; they gave no reason for thinking this. Eudoxus, without comment, had a fixed earth in the middle of the universe. Aristotle decided that the earth was held fixed at the centre of the universe by its natural tendency to be there. Aristarchus came to the opposite conclusion; according to Archimedes he supposed that the stars and the sun are fixed and that the earth revolves in a circle round the sun, the stars being so far away that the motion of the earth does not cause a detectable change in their apparent positions.

The definitive Greek treatment was by Ptolemy. He repeated Aristotle's reasoning, adding that if the earth were not at the centre of the universe the visible part of the heavens would not be a hemisphere. He said that if the earth moved birds would be left hanging in the air and would quickly fall out of the sky. And if the earth spins on its axis anything thrown in the air would be left behind by the earth and would seem to move westwards.

The spinning of the earth on its axis and its revolution round the sun are two separate phenomena. Aryabhata believed that the earth spins (and that the stars are fixed) but does not move through space.

Ptolemy's reasoning held sway until Copernicus came to the opposite conclusion. Copernicus maintained that the rotation of the earth on its axis is 'natural'. Here he was following Aristotle's distinction between natural and unnatural motion, though to Aristotle natural motion was in a circle for heavenly bodies and in a straight line for earthly bodies. Copernicus added that the sky cannot rotate because the immensity of the motion would be infinite and anything infinite cannot be moved. In any case, he said, stillness is more godlike than motion and should belong to the sky rather than to the earth.

This reasoning does not make a lot of sense. Copernicus fell well short of proving that the earth moves round the sun, and the popular belief that he did so simply isn't true. Galileo saw that this reasoning was no good, and tried to bolster it by reasons of his own, maintaining that the tides were caused by the movement of the earth, like water sloshing round in a tub carried in a cart. This, too, is wrong: tides are caused by the gravitational pull of the moon, and even though the theory of gravitation had not then been discovered, Galileo should have known that tides have a monthly cycle.

Galileo had an interesting answer to the argument that, if the earth moved, anything dropped from a height would not fall straight down, but would deviate by the distance that the surface of the earth moved while the object was falling. Today we know that if you drop a peanut in an airliner it does not fly to the back of the cabin. Galileo, who did not have such a striking example at his disposal, suggested shutting yourself up in the cabin of a ship moving as fast as you like, as long as the motion is smooth. He said that you will see that drops of water fall exactly into the mouth of a jar placed underneath, a ball thrown to and fro behaves exactly as if the ship were still, and butterflies fly equally well in all directions and are not pinned to the aft bulkhead. He added that he had made the experiment, but even before that natural reason had firmly persuaded him that the things had to happen in the way that they in fact do. This last remark arouses the suspicion that wishful thinking might have played a part. Galileo might have reported what he knew in his heart ought to happen rather than what he actually saw. A sailing-ship in a stiff breeze does not move smoothly and the movement of a hard-rowed vessel is definitely jerky. I wouldn't be too sanguine about catching drops of water on a fast yacht, and if the ship is moving slowly the observed phenomena don't prove anything. The behaviour of the butterfly doesn't prove anything in any case, because the air in the cabin is being carried along with the cabin.

A few years later Pierre Gassendi claimed to have dropped stones from the mast of a trireme travelling on a calm sea fast enough to cover four miles in a quarter of an hour. He was surprised that the stone fell at the foot of the mast. I would be surprised, too. If the stone is dropped while the oars are swinging forwards between strokes, when of course the ship is losing speed, the stone will fall in front of the mast; if it is dropped during the stroke, the stone will fall behind the mast. But I must admit that I have not actually found a trireme and made the experiment.

Ironically, the rotation of the earth does make falling objects deviate from the vertical, though the deviation is small: 1 centimetre in a fall of 70 metres.

If the reasons put forward by Copernicus and Galileo were so unsound, why did a system in which planets, including the earth, encircled a stationary sun prevail over the others?

Not because the earth goes round the sun rather than the sun round the earth. It was because Copernicus put the solar system together in a sensible way. Ptolemy's system had five unexplained coincidences: the lines from the mean sun to the centres of the epicycles of Mars, Jupiter and Saturn, and the lines from the earth to the centres of the epicycles of Venus and Mercury are all parallel to the line from the earth to the mean sun. Aryabhata's system had similar unexplained coincidences.

Copernicus's system explains all five coincidences. However, a system in which the sun goes round a stationary earth while the planets circle the moving sun would explain them equally well. Brahe proposed such a system but it did not become popular. Perhaps it looked too much like the tail wagging the dog.

Today we know that the sun is not stationary – it is moving round the centre of our galaxy. Is the centre of the galaxy stationary? The question is meaningless: all motion is relative.

TIDES

SOMETIMES, on the seashore near where I live, the sea comes right up to where the grass and other vegetation is growing; at other times the water is well away from there, uncovering several hundred metres of sand and mud – high tide and low tide. In fact, tides are spectacular; early people – at least those who lived near a shore – must have been well aware of them.

I live on the edge of the Pacific ocean. The Mediterranean is a relatively small sea and the tides there are quite negligible. So people who lived there might not have been so familiar with tides. The Greeks, however, knew of tides beyond the straits of Gibraltar.

What might early people have wanted to know about tides? Some would have wanted to find out what causes them. Other, more practical people, such as sailors, would want to be able to predict the times of high and low tide. To do this, they would need to find out as much detail about tides as they could.

Today we know that tides are caused by the gravitational pull of the moon and, to a lesser extent, of the sun. Before the discovery of gravitation it was not possible to explain the cause of tides. This did not stop people from trying.

Some odd suggestions were made about the cause of tides. The early Indians put them down to the breathing of a monstrous sea-god. Aristotle attributed the tides just beyond Gibraltar to the rockiness of the coast. William Gilbert, who discovered magnetism, said (about AD 1600) that they were due to magnetic attraction. Galileo, about the same date, said that they were caused by the motion of the earth.

As early as around 100 BC Posidonius noticed that the tides corresponded to the motion of the heavenly bodies (presumably he meant the sun and the moon). He described the daily changes in some detail: the tide begins to rise shortly after moonrise, reaches its height when the moon reaches its height, and then ebbs until just before the moon sets. It rises and falls in the same way between moonset and the next moonrise. He also described the monthly change : the range of the tide is greatest at new moon and full moon, least at half-moon. He finally described a yearly change: he said that the range was greatest at the solstices and least at the equinoxes. He was wrong: the range is (very slightly) greatest at the equinoxes. However, Pliny the elder got it right. He said not only that tides were greater at the equinoxes, but they were greater at the autumn equinox than the spring equinox. (And less at the summer solstice than the winter solstice.) He also noted that the highest tides were not exactly at new moon or full moon but a little later.

The Chinese recognized in the first century AD that the tides were related to the movement of the moon.

The venerable Bede (about AD 700) gave some figures: in twelve months the tide rises and falls 684 times. He also noticed that the tides where he lived, at Jarrow, in Northumbria, were later than the tides further north and earlier than those further south.

The earliest tide-tables known are from China, and were produced in 1054. They were for the tidal bore on the Chian Tang river. The earliest European tables, twelfth century AD, gave rules for the time of local high tide at full moon and added four-fifths of an hour for each day after then until the next full moon. Sailors, however, preferred to use the direction of the moon: one document says that a south-west or north-east moon gives high tide at London bridge.

Predicting tides is a complicated business: the tide is not highest when the moon is at its height but lags behind it by an amount depending, among other things, on the shape of the shoreline. But a combination of modern theories of hydrodynamics and a meticulous record of past tides enables reliable tide tables to be produced.

6

The Universe

THE BABYLONIANS and some early Greek astronomers, Hipparchus for example, investigated the motions of individual celestial bodies but did not try to combine them into a complete system. However, Aristotle built Eudoxus's model into a complete system; Ptolemy devised a complete system, not in the *Syntaxis* but in a later work; Aryabhata had a complete system; and the Chinese had at least two systems.

The earliest thinker, as far as we know, to try to put the universe – or at least the sun, moon and stars – together is Anaximander, born shortly before 600 BC. Only a few fragments of his writings have survived but they give us some idea of his views. He noted that the sun, moon and stars make, in the course of a whole day, a complete circle round the earth (he seems to have ignored stars too near the pole to set). This would be impossible if the earth were 'solid all the way down' as naive common sense might suggest, or floating in water, as some earlier philosophers thought. Anaximander stated clearly that the earth is floating freely in space, not tempted to change its position because it is at the centre of everything. He thought that it is shaped like one of the cylindrical segments from which Greek columns were constructed. Its height is one-third of its diameter, and we live on one of the flat sides. The sun is actually a circular tube 27 times (though one fragment says 28 times) as big as the earth. It is filled with fire, and what we see as the sun is a hole in the tube. If it were not for the dampness of the atmosphere, the heat of the sun would burn us all up. The moon's tube is 19 times as big as the earth (and presumably filled with something that gives off a silvery glow) and the hole in it changes shape to give the phases of the moon. The stars are pin-holes in fiery tubes that encircle the earth like the bark round a tree. (So presumably Anaximander thought that they lie on a cylindrical surface, though one fragment mentions the sphere of the stars.) The stars are nearest the earth and the sun furthest away. This is the first known attempt to build a universe with numerical measurements.

Aristotle's version of Eudoxus's system had no numerical dimensions.

In it the outermost sphere for Saturn is the celestial sphere and Jupiter's spheres fit inside Saturn's. But Saturn's innermost sphere is not moving like the celestial sphere and therefore will not serve as an outermost sphere for Jupiter. So Aristotle had to introduce, inside the spheres for Saturn, spheres which rotate about the same axes as Saturn's spheres but in opposite directions in order to cancel their motions, until he had a sphere which moved like the celestial sphere and could serve as an outermost sphere for Jupiter. He fitted Mars, Venus, the sun and the moon into the system in the same way.

Ptolemy thought that there was no wasted space in the sky: the least distance of Mercury from the earth was the greatest distance of the moon, the least distance of Venus was the greatest distance of Mercury, and so on. After Venus came the sun, Mars, Jupiter, Saturn and the stars in that order. His theories told him the ratio of the greatest to the least distances of each planet. From his estimate (quite a good one) for the distance of the moon he was able to calculate what the distances of the other heavenly bodies would be if his theory were correct. He also had, separately, a terribly bad estimate of the distance of the sun. By an unfortunate coincidence, the distance computed from his erroneous theory was so close to this estimate that he thought that his theory was confirmed.

Eudoxus had the moon nearest the earth, then the sun, Mercury, Venus, Mars, Jupiter, Saturn and the stars. Ptolemy also had the moon first and the planets in the same order but he had the sun between Venus and Mars. It was not possible, even in Ptolemy's time, to find the distance of any of these bodies except the moon, because only the moon showed perceptible parallax. The fact that the moon is nearest is confirmed by the fact that it eclipses the others: Aristotle, for example, saw it eclipsing Mars.

Although the planets all move close to the ecliptic they are so small that they rarely eclipse each other, and we have no ancient reports of such eclipses. However, in AD 1590 Kepler saw Mars eclipse Jupiter. The red colour of Mars showed, proving that Mars was the nearer of the two. In AD 1591 he saw Venus eclipse Mars. The white colour of Venus showed, proving that Venus was the nearer of the two.

From the modern point of view there is no sense in talking of the distance of the planets from the earth: Mercury for example is at times much nearer to us than is Venus, but at other times much further away.

Aryabhata assumed that the speeds of the moon, the sun and the planets were all the same. He was able to consider the actual speeds because he thought of the earth as spinning and the celestial sphere as still. It follows that the sizes of the planets' orbits were proportional to their sidereal periods:

if one planet has an orbit, say, four times as big as another's, it will have a sidereal period four times as long. (Unlike the Greeks, Aryabhata incorporated into his system the sidereal periods of Venus and Mercury, that is, the times taken for them to revolve once round the sun, as explained on page 79.) From the sidereal periods and the size of the moon's orbit he could calculate the sizes of the other orbits. The idea that there is a strict relation between the size of the orbit and the sidereal period is correct, but the relation is not what Aryabhata thought: if one planet has an orbit four times as big as another's, it will have a sidereal period not four but eight times as long. The sidereal period is proportional to the size of the orbit multiplied by its square root.

We must distinguish between systems like the ones that I have been describing, which are based on reasoning (admittedly unsound reasoning), on one hand and on the other purely speculative theories, usually called 'cosmologies': for example, the theory of the later followers of Pythagoras that the earth revolved round a central fire, shielded from it by an anti-earth. Such theories belong to mythology rather than to astronomy. Whether the modern 'big bang' cosmology truly belongs in astronomy is something that bears thinking about.

The Chinese had two main theories. I mentioned the *gai tian* theory earlier. *Gai* means 'lid' or 'cover'; *tian* means 'sky'. One reference said 'the square earth is a chariot; the round sky its canopy'. Another said that the sky is like a rain-hat and the earth like an upturned pan. (So we don't know whether these early Chinese thought that the earth was round or square.) Ancient Chinese pans had fairly flat bases and curved sides; some chariots' canopies in bas-reliefs of the Han period had flattish tops.

The *Zhou bi* gave a few dimensions.

The point on the earth below the pole is 60,000 *li* higher than the inhabited part of the earth. The centre of the sky is 60,000 *li* higher than its edges. The sky is 80,000 *li* from the earth. When the sun is furthest from the pole (in winter) it is 20,000 *li* higher than the land below the pole. These figures clash badly with the computational part of the *Zhou bi*, which assumes that the earth is flat.

The *Zhou bi* stated that when the sun is in its central orbit its illumination extends up to the pole, but almost immediately contradicted this by saying that the illumination extends 167,000 *li* on all sides, which makes it fall 11,500 *li* short of the pole. 11,500 *li* is also the radius of the orbit of a star called *xuan ji*, literally 'revolving pivot'. Its orbit was measured by sighting its furthest east and west displacements using the gnomon-and-string method. This star may be mythical.

The total region illuminated by the sun has a diameter of 810,000 *li*, and no one knows what is beyond this. Possibly 810,000 is an auspicious number; one commentator describes 81 as the ultimate *yang* number.

The second main Chinese theory, called *hun tian* ('celestial sphere'), goes back to at least 100 BC. It likens the sky to an egg with the earth as its yolk, floating on water. The part above the earth is filled with vapour. One difficulty with this theory is that the sun and the stars would have to move through the water as they orbit the earth.

If the egg were spherical this theory would tie in nicely with the use of armillary spheres as astronomical instruments, and one commentator quoted this as one of its advantages. The orbits of the heavenly bodies were regarded as circles on the sphere, the path of the sun being called the yellow path and the path of the moon the white path. The red path is not an orbit but the celestial equator.

7

Dates and Times

TIME

Although the Mayas worked only in whole days most people divided the day into smaller units. The Babylonians divided it into twelve units called *beru*, each equal to two of our hours. For a smaller unit they used a thirtieth of a *beru*, which they called an *ush*. They also had a popular system, which divided the night into twelve equal parts. Because nights vary in length according to the season of the year, so do these parts: we call them seasonal hours. By contrast, one twenty-fourth of a noon-to-noon day is an equinoctial hour.

The Egyptian decans (explained on page 49) divided the night into 16 parts, but by allowing for twilight the Egyptians came to divide it into twelve, giving them seasonal hours.

The Greeks used equinoctial hours, which they divided into sixtieths, sixtieths-of-sixtieths and so on. When Ptolemy used Babylonian observations with the time quoted in hours he took the hours to be seasonal and started by converting them to equinoctial hours.

The Chinese astronomers divided the day into a hundred equal parts called *ke*. The Chinese had another system in which the day was divided into twelve *shi* (so a *shi* was equal to a Babylonian *beru*, presumably by coincidence). These were given the names of twelve 'earthly branches' and midnight was in the middle of the first, so, for example, the fifth, *chen*, started 3½ *shi* after midnight (which is 29 *ke* to the nearest whole *ke*). The astronomers calculated that a certain solstice occurred 32 *ke* after midnight. They quoted this in an almanac as *chen 3 ke*.

You can tell how time passes by watching the heavens rotate. Every Boy Scout and Girl Guide knows how to find the Pole Star by following the two stars in the Big Dipper known as the pointers, and will have noticed how they turn. The Babylonians sometimes pinpointed events by using this rotation, for example by saying what star was just rising on the horizon when the event occurred.

The turning of the shadow of a gnomon also marks the passage of time. If, instead of using a vertical gnomon, we use one pointing to the celestial pole, with a base-plate at right angles to it, we have a sundial whose shadow turns at a nearly constant rate.

Most early people also had water clocks. A vase with a hole in the bottom is filled with water and by measuring the water that leaks out in an interval we can tell how long the interval is. The Chinese had some elaborate water clocks with ingenious devices to keep the water level always the same and so prevent the rate of leakage from varying.

In the eighth century AD the Chinese invented clockwork, and eventually this reached the west. But early clocks were not very accurate and as late as the sixteenth century Brahe preferred to time things astronomically.

The Arabs had tables for calculating the time from the date and the elevation of the sun.

Noon is determined as the time when the sun is due south. This is what we call nowadays 'local noon' because the sun is due south of different places at different times. The Greeks knew this and knew how to allow for it.

There is a complication. Partly because the motion of the sun is irregular, and partly because its orbit is slanting, the time from noon to noon (at the same place) is not always the same. To even this out, astronomers define *mean local noon* to be the time when the sun would be due south if it moved at constant rate in an orbit parallel to the plane of the equator. Time measured from local noon – the time shown by a sundial – is solar time. Time measured from mean local noon is mean solar time. The difference between them is called the equation of time. (From the Latin *equatio*, meaning what has to be added or subtracted in order to equalize.) Ptolemy was able to apply the equation of time.

A CHINESE CYCLE

JUST AS WE have a cycle of seven days – the days of the week – that repeats over and over again independently of the date, the Chinese had a cycle of sixty days. Each of the sixty days is described by two characters: one of the ten 'heavenly trunks' followed by one of the twelve 'earthly branches'. The sequence is completely known. For example *xin-hai* is 48th in the cycle, *ji-chou* is 26th, 22 days earlier.

The two solstices mentioned on page 13 occurred on

xin-hai in the first month of the fifth year of Xi gong

and on

ji-chou in the second month of the twentieth year of Zhao gong,

so the number of days between them is 22 less than a multiple of 60. We know enough Chinese history to identify the years as 655 BC and 522 BC. The difference is 133, so the number of days between the solstices must be close to 133 times 365¼. 48,578 fills the bill.

The Chinese used the sixty-year cycle to number years, too. Today they use only the twelve branches; this gives us the year of the dragon (chen), the year of the tiger (yin) and so on. (The characters used for the branches are special ones; the ordinary Chinese words for 'dragon' and 'tiger' are quite different characters, pronounced long and hu.)

INDIAN PERIODS

MEDIEVAL INDIAN astronomers believed in a long period of time called a kalpa at whose beginning and end the sun, the moon, the mean planets, the apogees, the sighras, the moon's descending node – in fact, just about everything – had longitude zero. The length of the kalpa is 4,320 million years.

One ten thousandth of a kalpa is a kali yuga, and the start of the current kali yuga has been identified as 3102 BC, February 18th in the Julian calendar.

The earliest firmly-dated work using this principle that has come down to us is the Aryabhatiya, compiled by Aryabhata, who was born in AD 476. He gave the numbers of revolutions in a basic period of the sun, the moon, the moon's nodes and apogee, the mean outer planets, and the sighras of Venus and Mercury.

From the number of revolutions of the sun, namely 4,320,000, we can see that the basic period is ten kali yugas.

The sun, the moon, the outer planets, and the sighras of the inner planets each made a whole number of revolutions between the start of the kalpa and the start of the current kali yuga.

Aryabhata did not explain how his figures were to be used, but later commentators did. To find, say, the longitude of an outer planet at a certain date, we first calculate the number of days between this date and the start of the kali yuga. If we divide this number by the number of days in the basic period and multiply by the number of revolutions of the mean planet in the basic period we obtain the number of revolutions of the mean planet since the start of the kali yuga. The fractional part, converted from revolutions to degrees, gives the mean longitude at the date we are interested in. We find the longitude of the *sighra* of the planet, which is the mean longitude of the sun, in the same way. Knowing these, we can compute the longitude of the planet.

8

Calendars

CALENDARS ARE NOT IMPORTANT in the development of astronomy, but astronomy is important in the development of the calendar. The desire to produce a calendar was probably one reason why the Babylonians and the ancient Greeks studied closely the solstices and new moons. Let us look at the various kinds of calendar.

COUNTING THE DAYS

DAYS have probably been counted informally many times – a prisoner marking off the days on the wall of his or her cell, for example. It has been done formally twice. The Mayas had a count of days, called the *long count* by western historians, from a zero date well in the past. And our Julian day (nothing to do with the Julian calendar) is also a simple count of days. The disadvantage here is that we run into enormous numbers: the year AD 1 started on Julian day 1,721,424. So we group the days.

GROUPING THE DAYS

Do we group the days in sevens and number the weeks? No, though British ration-books in the second world war came close to this. Did the Chinese group the days in sixties, using their well-known sixty-day cycle (described earlier) and number the cycles? No: they could have, but they didn't. The Mayas grouped the days into *tuns*, a *tun* being 360 days. (See appendix 2, p.105) The Maya long count 10.02.10.11.07 is *tun* 10.02.10, day 11.07 (i.e. *tun* 4050, day 227), so the numbers are not as horrendous as if it were a pure count of days, which would be 1,458,227. Far and away the commonest grouping was into years (cycles of the sun) and months (cycles of the moon).

USING THE SUN AND MOON

THEORETICALLY we could have a pure lunar calendar: group the days into months and number the months. But nobody did this. Most people realized that there were just over twelve months in a year and gave them twelve names (except for the Chinese, who numbered them). Anthropologists have even found examples of primitive tribes doing this. The Islamic calendar formally makes a year equal to twelve months and numbers the years. This makes their year about eleven days shorter than everyone else's year.

The Babylonians and the Chinese realized that the year is substantially longer than twelve months, and inserted an extra month from time to time to allow for this. The Babylonians did not have an extra name: they repeated one of the twelve names. And the Chinese repeated one of the twelve numbers.

To begin with, the extra month was inserted whenever it seemed necessary; perhaps grain ripened in a later month than usual, or the rainy season came in the wrong month, or a heliacal rising was late. But it is obviously convenient to be able to tell in advance how the calendar will go.

The Chinese, Babylonians and Greeks all found a 19-year relation. The Chinese called it *zhang*, the Greeks called it the Metonic cycle. It gave rise to a series of nineteen years of which seven contained thirteen months to give the right total – 12 12 13 12 12 13 12 13 12 12 13 12 12 13 12 12 13 12 13 – repeated over and over again.

It is still used today. If you look up the instructions in the book of common prayer for finding the date of Easter you will find it there.

IGNORING THE MOON

THE EGYPTIANS and the Romans gave up these complications, and the Mayas never had them. All three based their calendars simply on the length of the year.

The Egyptian and Mayan years were each 365 days long, and get out of step with the seasons by about one day every four years, as mentioned earlier.

Neither the Mayas nor the Egyptians numbered the days in the year right through. The Mayas divided the years into eighteen named periods of twenty days each plus five extra days. The Egyptians divided the year into twelve named periods of thirty days each (which we, somewhat misleadingly, call months) plus five extra days.

Having the first day of the year move through the seasons seems to have bothered Julius Caesar, so he made every fourth year a leap year, giving us the Julian calendar used throughout most of European history. It is divided up in the crazy thirty-days-hath-September method familiar to us all. It gets out of step with the seasons at the rate of one day every 128 years.

This was good enough for everyone except the Church, which was worried, not about the seasons, but about the date of Easter.

So in 1582 pope Gregory XIII introduced the Gregorian calendar, which has 97 leap years every 400 years. This was gradually adopted throughout the world, though some nations, Iran for example, still use their own calendars as well. It will be a long time before it needs to be adjusted.

NUMBERING THE YEARS

SOMETIMES A YEAR is identified by naming an event that took place in it, for example, the year when Apseudes was archon of Athens (which was actually 432 BC). A common method is to number the years in the reign of the ruler or of the dynasty, for example Cambyses 7 (Persian) or Yuan 6 (Chinese). This method was used until recently in England for dating legal cases. The Chinese sometimes used individual reigns instead of dynasties, and sometimes divided a reign into smaller periods numbered separately.

The Greeks had a cycle of 76 years called the Callipic cycle. The first one started at the summer solstice of 329 BC. So the fourth year of the first cycle started in 325 BC, the first year of the second cycle started in 253 BC, and so on.

But the best way is to fix on some date and number the years from then on. For example, Roman years were numbered from the supposed founding of the city: *ab urbe conditum.*

Persia had the Seleucid era, starting in 310 BC, our AD dates start at the supposed date of the birth of Jesus Christ, the Indian Saka period starts in AD 78, and the Islamic calendar starts with the flight of Mohammed to Medina, in AD 622.

For more details on calendars, including detailed instructions on how to convert one to another, I thoroughly recommend *Mapping Time* by E. G. Richards.

MODERN DEVELOPMENTS

GALILEO and his telescopes bring us to a watershed in the investigation of the universe. He found that Venus has phases; it is sometimes nearly full, sometimes a crescent, so its orbit cannot be between us and the sun. Ptolemy and Aryabhata were wrong. Copernicus (and Brahe) could be right.

Later, more powerful telescopes enabled us to see three new planets, to recognise that the Milky Way consists of a large number of stars too small to be distinguished by the naked eye, and to recognize that certain fuzzy objects, the nebulas, are actually distant galaxies. We end up with a highly technological astronomy using spectroscopes, radio-telescopes, laser beams and spacecraft.

At the same time as Galileo, Kepler was starting an equally fundamental but more theoretical revolution. He found the true shape of the orbits – they are ellipses – and the law regulating the speed round the orbit. This opened the way for Newton's theory of gravitation and his laws of motion to explain all heavenly movement to a high degree of accuracy – accurate enough for the tiny effect of one planet on another to enable astronomers to predict the existence of Uranus, then Neptune, and then Pluto. However, we had to wait for Einstein's theory of general relativity to obtain complete (as far as we know at present) accuracy. Only for Mercury is the difference between motion according to Newton and motion according to Einstein big enough to be detected.

These recent advances, so briefly sketched above, are too technical for detailed description here. The best source for more details is a textbook of astronomy.

WHY ASTRONOMY?

WHY DID EARLY PEOPLE study astronomy? One possible reason, which many writers on the topic underemphasize, is sheer intellectual curiosity – the very human desire to know whatever can be known. After all, that is the only reason to dig up dinosaurs, send a spacecraft to the far side of the moon, or prove Fermat's last theorem.

Having found that the cycle of the sun, whether from highest to lowest elevation at noon and back, or from most northerly to most southerly position on the horizon and back, is always the same length of time, it is natural to try to find out exactly how long it is. And when people discovered the peculiar back-and-forth motion of the planets, why not try to get a grip on the details?

But there are also some practical benefits from astronomy. Whether people studied astronomy in its own right and the benefits followed, or whether they studied it for the sake of the benefits we shall probably never know. I expect that it is a bit of each.

If the Greeks followed Hesiod, they used heliacal risings to tell them when to reap or sow. If the Incas followed their astronomers' instructions they used the date of the solstice to this end. And the Hopis used the position of the sunrise not only to do this but to set the date of festivals.

You can use astronomy to find your way. Every Boy Scout and Girl Guide knows how to find the Pole Star, which gives them the direction of north. Geographers (even the Chinese, who did not know that the earth is round) used the elevation of the pole to tell how far north or south a place is. Navigators did this, too (right up to the invention of the Global Positioning Satellite). And we have seen how islanders in the Pacific ocean used the stars to navigate.

The Babylonians made great practical use of their study of the moon. They could predict the times of moonrise and moonset, and the dates of new moon and full moon – important in the days before street-lighting. (And important even today, for example to Bomber Command in the Second World War.) Here is a fairly clear case where astronomy was studied for practical purposes.

Having studied the moon intensively they found that they could predict eclipses. There is little practical importance to this (except for companies which arrange tours to places where an eclipse of the sun is total) but Columbus made ingenious use of this ability. On February 29th 1504 he was stranded in Jamaica. The natives refused to supply him with provisions. He knew that there would be an eclipse of the moon early that evening, and threatened to destroy the moon if the natives did not relent. When the eclipse started, they relented.

Astronomy can be used to tell the time. The ancient Greeks, Babylonians and Vedic astronomers had tables giving, for various dates in the year, the lengths of the shadow of a gnomon at various intervals before and after noon. The rotation of the shadow can also be used: we now have a sundial. The dial itself can be horizontal, on the ground, or vertical, on a wall (using a horizontal rod to cast the shadow). Best of all is to have the dial parallel to the plane of the equator and the rod perpendicular to it. The risings and settings of stars can be used: if you tell an astronomer which star is just rising or setting (on a given date) he or she can tell you the time of night. Equally well, you could say which star is due south of you. And we have seen how to use the astrolabe to tell the time.

Another practical benefit was the ability to produce a luni-solar calendar, though this needs only the study of the dates of solstices and new moons.

Is there a practical use for a study of the planets? Brahe used Venus to find the longitudes of stars. And after Galileo had discovered the satellites of Jupiter their positions could be used to tell the time. By comparing this with local time, found by using the sun, an explorer could find his longitude. But far and away the main use for the study of the planets was in astrology.

There is only one practical use for astrology that I have ever heard of; it is said that during the Second World War British astrologers were able to tell the government what advice Hitler was getting from his astrologers. (Anyone who has compared horoscopes from two different newspapers could be excused for being sceptical about the value of this.)

It remains true, however, that many astronomers, including Hipparchus, Ptolemy and Kepler, believed in astrology. Once people had noticed that the sun controls the seasons and the length of daylight it became natural to wonder whether the other heavenly bodies control anything on earth. Two things that are controlled by the moon were not known to either Chinese or western astronomers. The palolo worm in the Pacific ocean breeds only when the moon is in its last quarter, and the grunion in California and Baja California spawns only on the three or four days after a full moon or new moon – a truly spectacular sight. (Obviously the moon's influence on the tides is at work here.)

But whatever the motives for investigating the planets, the result, whether that of the Babylonians or Ptolemy or, above all, the final result due to Kepler, is one of the great triumphs of the human intellect.

Further Reading

A BOOK WHICH COVERS the same ground as this and gives complete references is my *Early Astronomy* (1994, paperback 1996). Warning: this book contains a fair amount of mathematics.

Astronomy Before the Telescope (1996) is beautifully illustrated and covers also some primitive African and Australian astronomy.

The classical general work is J. L. E. Dreyer's *The History of the Planetary System from Thales to Kepler* (1906, reprinted in 1953 as *The History of Astronomy ...*), outdated but very readable.

For Babylonian astronomy I recommend the delightfully-written chapter in Otto Neugebauer's *The Exact Sciences in Antiquity* (1957), and the second volume of B. L. van der Waerden's *Science Awakening* (1974).

Neugebauer's *History of Ancient Mathematical Astronomy* (1975) covers Babylonian and Greek astronomy in painstaking detail.

For Chinese astronomy there is volume 3 of Joseph Needham's *Science and Civilization in China* (1954). An excellent treatment of early Chinese astronomy, with a complete translation of an important early treatise is Christopher Cullen's *Astronomy and Mathematics in Ancient China: the Zhou bi suan jing* (1996).

There are translations of two Indian works: K. S. Shukla's *The Aryabhatiya of Aryabhata* (1976) and Bina Chatterjee's *The Khandakhadyaka of Brahmagupta* (1970). In French there is Roger Billard's *L'astronomie Indienne* (1971).

The classical source for early Greek astronomy is Sir Thomas Heath's *Aristarchus of Samos, the Ancient Copernicus: a History of Greek Astronomy* to *Aristarchus* (1913, reprinted 1981). This can be supplemented by D. R. Dicks's *Early Greek Astronomy to Aristotle* (1970).

The orthodox view of Ptolemy is tellingly, if somewhat polemically, challenged in R. R. Newton's *The Crime of Claudius Ptolemy* (1977).

A good source for Aztec and Maya astronomy is Anthony Aveni's *Skywatchers* (2001). This can be supplemented by John Teeple's *Mayan Astronomy* (1930) and J. E. S. Thompson's *A Commentary on the Dresden Codex* (1972).

The Dictionary of Scientific Biography (1978) gives useful details of the work of those astronomers who are included.

The *Griffith Observer*, published by the Griffith observatory in Los Angeles, has many articles on the history of astronomy. It also has a Sky Calendar each month, which gives the reader a clear idea of what can be seen with the naked eye (it tells you when you need binoculars or a telescope) from one place on the earth's surface.

Appendix 1

BABYLONIAN NUMERALS

THE BABYLONIANS wrote by pressing a stylus into a clay tablet, making impressions in the shape of wedges, which gave this method of writing the name *cuneiform*.

For numbers up to sixty the Babylonians used a stroke for 1 and a vee for 10. To them, our 23 was:

For numbers greater than sixty they used a system like our decimal system but based on sixty instead of ten. Just as to us 63 means 6 tens plus 3, so to a Babylonian:

meant 2 sixties plus 23 (143 in our notation). Historians replace strokes and vees by our digits, writing the number above as 2,23.

To deal with fractions, Babylonians routinely divided a unit of weight, length, time etc. into sixtieths, so where we would have 2¼ they would have 2,15 (2 and 15 sixtieths). This principle enabled them to describe fractions to a high degree of precision. For example, a table giving the calculated longitude of a new moon contains an entry 2, 2, 6,20. This represents 2 + 2/60 + 6/60× 60 + 20/60× 60× 60.

Although I have heard that since we switched to the decimal system the commonest mistake in dispensing is getting a dose wrong by a factor of 10, the context normally shows what number is meant. When I buy pork chops and the butcher says 'That'll be three seventy-five' I know that he means $3.75, not $375. Similarly, when a Babylonian saw 2, 15 he would know from the context whether it meant 2¼ or 135.

The Babylonians had a separation sign (which I shall denote by oo) that was used to distinguish between, say 2, 15 (i.e. 135) and 2, oo, 15 (i.e. 7215).

Incidentally, the Greek astronomer Ptolemy also used fractions to the base 60. The Greeks did not, of course, use cuneiform wedges. Instead they used Greek letters for digits, $\alpha = 1$, $\beta = 2$ etc.; $\iota = 10$, $\kappa = 20$ etc. So $\kappa\alpha = 21$.

Appendix 2

MAYAN NUMERALS

AYAN NUMERALS are easy to read. A dot counts as 1, a bar as 5, and a shell as zero, so the two dots and three bars at the bottom of column 1 in figure 29 (p. 62) are the Mayan numeral for 17. The three dots and one bar just above are the Mayan numeral for 8. When two numerals occur together like this, the upper one counts twenties so the two numerals between them represent the Mayan way of writing 8 twenties plus 17, i.e. 177.

When three Mayan numerals appear together, the top one counts 360s. The reason for this is astronomical. The only examples that we have of long chains of Mayan numerals are counts of days. The Mayas had a unit of time called a *tun* (we can deduce the pronunciation from surviving Mayan languages) which equals 360 days, presumably chosen to be the nearest multiple of 20 to the number of days in a year. So in a long chain of numerals the last two numerals count days, the preceding ones count *tuns*. The number at the top of column 6 denotes 2 *tuns* 313 days. If there are more than three numerals the last one counts single days; the one before it counts twenties of days; the one before that counts *tuns*; the one before that counts twenties of *tuns* – twenty *tuns* is called a *katun*. From then on each numeral counts a unit twenty times as big as the one after it.

There are a few mistakes in figure 29: for example the top numeral in column 1 should have three dots. The table as a whole is so regular that it is no trouble to put these mistakes right.

Appendix 3

CHINESE HAS A CHARACTER for each digit. The characters act both as our digits 1 to 9 and our words 'one' to 'nine'. There are also characters for ten, hundred, thousand, and so on.

Modern Chinese has a method for spelling these characters in Roman letters.

A typical large number is

yi	qian	liu	bai	ju	shi	wu
1	thousand	6	hundred	9	ten	5

This denotes 1,695 in our notation.

Chinese indicates fractions by using the character *fen*, which literally means 'division' and *zhi*, a character with no intrinsic meaning which grammarians call a particle. For example, a *bu* is a unit of length and *wu, fen, bu, zhi* denotes one-fifth (*wu* = 5) of a *bu*, and *wu, fen, bu, zhi, si* denotes four-fifths of a *bu* (*si* = 4). Zero is denoted by *kong*, which literally means 'empty'.

A few later Chinese almanacs, notably the *Yuan shi* of just before AD 1300 omitted the 'hundred', 'thousand' and so on. This is perhaps the inspiration for (or perhaps it was inspired by) the Indian decimal system described in appendix 4.

Appendix 4

INDIAN NUMERALS

THE INDIANS had several ways of representing numbers. They had ten digits which are the origin of both our so-called arabic numerals and the real arabic numerals that you can see on number plates in Cairo.

The Indians also represented numbers by words, using things that naturally occur in pairs, such as eyes or hands, to represent 2, for instance, or 'space' to represent zero. This system is much less vulnerable than the digits to miscopying or to wear and tear on old documents. It also gave more flexibility to the writer, who needed it because Indian astronomical treatises were often in verse.

Sanskrit is written from left to right. The number-words start with the units digit, then the tens digit, and so on. This means that they are in what we would call reverse order. For example,

twenty-two million, nine hundred and sixty-eight thousand, two hundred and eighty-five

might be written (in Sanskrit script, of course) as

sarastapaksavasurasanavadviyamah.

Here *sara* stands for five, *asta* is the Sanskrit for eight, *paksa* stands for two, *vasu* stands for eight, *rasa* stands for six, *nava* is the Sanskrit for nine, and *dviyama* indicates two twos, *dvi* being the Sanskrit for two.

The first section of the *Aryabhatiya* uses yet another system. Numbers are represented by syllables. The first twenty-five consonants of the Sanskrit alphabet stand for the numbers from 1 to 25, and the next eight for the tens from 30 to 100. Each consonant is followed by a vowel: by the first vowel if it represents the units digit, by the second if it represents the hundreds digit, and so on.

For example, *kh* (two letters in our alphabet but one in Sanskrit) represents 2 and *u* is the third vowel, so *khu* represents 20,000.

Index